Excel

ADVANCED SKILLS

MATHS

YEAR
2
AGES
7–8

START
MATHS

Get the Results You Want!

PASCAL
PRESS

Damon James

© 2013 Pascal Press
Reprinted 2015

ISBN 978 1 74125 463 1

Pascal Press
PO Box 250
Glebe NSW 2037
(02) 8585 4044
www.pascalpress.com.au

Publisher: Vivienne Joannou
Edited by Gloria Harris and Chelsea Smithies
Typeset by Post Pre-Press
Cover by DiZign Pty Ltd
Printed by Green Giant Press

Contents

Unit 1 Numbers to 100   page 10

1 **Base ten blocks** are read as: short = 1 unit, long = 1 ten, flat = 1 hundred and cube = 1 thousand.

2 **Linking blocks (Unifix blocks)** are blocks that are joined together. They can be joined into groups of 10 to model place value situations.

3–4 A number can be written with **words** or **numerals** (digits) e.g. one hundred and fifty-five = 155.

Unit 2 Place value   page 10

1 **The place of a digit** in a number gives the value, e.g. in 57, 7 = 7 units and 5 = 5 tens

2 **Largest** and **smallest numbers** can be determined by first looking at the digits in the tens columns and comparing them. If they are the same, then look at the digits in the units column.

3 **Bundling sticks** are single sticks such as pop sticks that are grouped together to show bundles of 10. Then 10 groups can be put together to form 100.

4 The **next number** is found by counting on by 1. Note when 9 is reached, 1 is added to the units place making 0; therefore 1 is added to the tens place, e.g. the next number after 29 is 30.

Unit 3 Numbers to 1000   page 11

1 An **abacus** is read as the number of discs above each letter, where U = unit, T = tens and H = hundreds.

2 The **number of digits** is found by counting each separate digit, e.g. 25 has two digits and 250 has three digits.

3–4 See Unit 1 Nos 3–4

Unit 4 Ordering numbers (1)   page 11

1 See Unit 2 No. 1

2–3 See Unit 2 No. 2, then order once compared.

4 See Unit 2 No. 4

Unit 5 Ordering numbers (2)   page 12

1 To write the **smallest number**, find the smallest digit and write it first, then the next smallest and write it second and so on, e.g. using all the digits 5, 2, 7 the smallest number is 257.

2 To write the **largest number**, find the largest digit and write it first, then the next largest and write it second and so on, e.g. using the digits 1, 7, 5 the largest number is 751.

3–4 See Unit 2 No. 2

Unit 6 Counting forwards and backwards   page 12

1 See Unit 2 No. 4

2 Counting back by 1 gives the **number before**.

3 To **count forwards** start at the specified number, such as 10, and count on by the said number.

4 To **count backwards** start at the specified number, such as 10, and count back by the said number.

Unit 7 Expanding 2-digit numbers   page 13

1 A **number expander** shows values of numbers. The digit is written next to each value; units, tens etc.

| 9 | H | 5 | T | 6 | U | = 956 |

2 To **write the number**, take the first digit of each number and put them in order of place, e.g. 500 + 70 + 6 = 576, so the number is 576.

3 To **expand a number**, break the number into its components of hundreds, tens and units. Write it as an addition equation, e.g. 45 = 40 + 5

4 See Unit 2 No. 1

Unit 8 Expanding 3-digit numbers   page 13

1 See Unit 3 No. 1   2 See Unit 7 No. 2

3 See Unit 7 No. 3   4 See Unit 2 No. 1

Unit 9 Expanding 4-digit numbers   page 14

1 See Unit 7 No. 1   2 See Unit 2 No. 1

3 See Unit 7 No. 2   4 See Unit 7 No. 3

Unit 10 Ordering numbers (3)   page 14

1 See Unit 5 No. 2   2 See Unit 5 No. 1

3 See Unit 2 No. 2

4 See Unit 2 No. 1, then order once compared.

Unit 11 Simple addition   page 15

1 **Tens frames** are frames that provide structure for numbers up to 10, e.g.

$$\boxed{\begin{array}{cccc} \bullet & \bullet & \bullet & \bullet \\ \bullet & \bullet & \bullet & \end{array}} = 7$$

The **total** can be found by counting each of the dots (representing counters). Missing dots can be identified to total/make 10.

2 See Unit 1 No. 2, and these blocks can be counted to find the total number of blocks.

3 **Addition** is the combining of two or more numbers to make a larger one. This can be completed with numerals or words. Note: addition is the same as **add** or **sum** or **total** or **plus**. It can be completed by **counting on**.

4 **Open number lines** are lines with no scale that are used to show addition processes, e.g.

10 + 12 = 22

Unit 12 Counting on   page 15

1–3 See Unit 6 No. 3

4 See Unit 11 No. 4

Unit 13 Building to 10   page 16

1 See Unit 11 No. 1

2 See Unit 1 No. 2

3 **Missing numbers** can be found by counting on,
e.g.   14 + ☐ = 20
     14, 15, 16, 17, 18, 19, 20 is counting on 6.
So 14 + 6 = 20
Alternatively it is possible to say '14 + what = 20?'
The 'what' is 6.

4 By looking for **combinations of 10**, this makes addition easier, e.g. for 4 + 3 + 6
     4 + 6 = 10 and then 10 + 3 = 13
So 4 + 3 + 6 = 13

Unit 14 Doubles
page 16

1–3 Double is adding the same number. So double 4 is 4 + 4 which is 8, and double 5 is 10.

2 See Unit 6 No. 3.

4 See Unit 11 No. 3.

Unit 15 Tens facts
page 17

1 See Unit 11 No. 3

2 See Unit 14 Nos 1–3

3 Building to 10, can also be extended to 20, 30 and so on,
e.g. for 17 + ☐ = 20
Count on from 17 to find the value, i.e. 17, 18, 19, 20 which is counting on by 3.
So 17 + 3 = 20

4 Building to 10 can be extended to 100.
e.g.   40 + 50 + 50
50 + 50 = 100 then 100 + 40 = 140
So 40 + 50 + 50 = 140

Unit 16 Adding 10
page 17

1–3 See Unit 11 No. 3

4 Addition tables can be completed by adding each number to the number beside the +,
e.g.

+	12	22	32
10	(12+10)	(22+10)	(32+10)
	22	32	42

Unit 17 Commutative law
page 18

1–4 The **commutative law** in addition states that it doesn't matter which order the numbers are added in an addition equation, the answer will always be the same, e.g. 4 + 5 = 9 and 5 + 4 = 9. This reversibility can be used to find missing values.

Unit 18 Adding to 20
page 18

1 See Unit 2 No. 3 and Unit 11 No. 3

2–4 See Unit 11 No. 3

3 A **number sentence** is another name for an equation,
e.g. 5 + 4 = 9 is a number sentence.

Unit 19 Adding to 50
page 19

1 See Unit 11 No. 1, Unit 2 No. 3, Unit 3 No. 1, Unit 1 No. 2, Unit 11 No. 3 and Unit 18 No. 3.

2 See Unit 11 No. 3

3 See Unit 16 No. 4

4 See Unit 13 No. 3

Unit 20 Adding to 99
page 19

1 See Unit 2 No. 3 and Unit 11 No. 3

2–3 Addition can be completed **horizontally** or **vertically**.
Remember to line up units and tens in the correct columns,
e.g. 5 tens and 2 units + 3 tens and 1 unit
can be written as 5 + 3 tens and 2 + 1 units = 8 tens and 3 units or 83, e.g.

```
  5 t + 2 u              5 2
+ 3 t + 1 u     or     + 3 1
-----------            -----
  8 t + 3 u              8 3
```

4 See Unit 17 No. 3

Unit 21 Adding to 99 – vertically
page 20

1 See Unit 11 No. 3

2–3 See Unit 20: Nos 2–3

4 Missing numbers can be found by adding or counting on to make the total of each place value column,
e.g.

Unit 22 Adding 2 digit numbers
page 20

1 See Unit 11 No. 3 and Unit 20 Nos 2–3

2 See Unit 11 No. 3 and Unit 17 No. 3

3 The **jump strategy** is jumping along a number line by tens and then units to find the answer. This can also be completed mentally.
e.g.   44 + 23 =
Add tens first: 44 + 20 = 64
Then add the units: 64 + 3 = 67
So 44 + 23 = 67

4 The process of **adding three or more numbers** is the same as adding two numbers. See Unit 11 No. 3, Unit 15 Nos 3–4

Unit 23 Simple subtraction
page 21

1 Write the number at the start and subtract the number crossed out,
e.g. ⊠ ⊠ ☺ ☺ ☺ ☺ 6 – 2 = 4

2–4 Subtraction is the process of taking one quantity away from another. Subtract is the same as **take away** or **minus** or **difference**. A number line can aid the process of counting back to find the answer.
e.g.

20 – 13 = 7

Unit 24 Counting back
page 21

1–3 See Unit 6 No. 4

4 Open number lines can also be used to show subtraction processes. See Unit 23 Nos 2–4

Unit 25 Subtraction patterns
page 22

1 Use **crossing off** to work out how many left and notice the pattern of 'cross off one more, one less is left'.

2 and 4 Notice the **pattern** where the remainder has the same units answer even if the tens change.

3 Note that subtractions come in **pairs**.

Unit 26 10s facts
page 22

1 See Unit 11 No. 1. The empty spaces on a 10s frame can be counted to find the **difference**.

2 Counting on to 10 is a strategy to find the missing number.

3 See Unit 23 Nos 2–4

4 The **missing numbers** can be found by counting back.

Unit 27 **Subtraction 10** page 23

1–2 Subtracting 1 ten means taking 1 from the Tens place value column.
  e.g.   45 subtract 1 ten, is 40 – 10 = 30
      so 45 – 10 = 35

3 See Unit 24 No. 4

4 Subtraction tables can be completed by subtracting the number next to the – from the other listed numbers.
  e.g.

–	25	35	45
10	(25–10)	(35–10)	(45–10)
	15	25	35

Unit 28 **Subtraction to 20** page 23

1–2 and 4 See Unit 23 Nos 2–4

3 See Unit 24 No. 4

Unit 29 **Subtraction to 50** page 24

1 and 3 See Unit 23 Nos 2–4

2 The **jump strategy** is jumping along a number line by tens and then units to find the answer. This can also be completed mentally.
  e.g.   44 – 23 =
      Subtract tens first: 44 – 20 = 24
      Then subtract the units: 24 – 3 = 21
      So 44 – 23 = 21

4 Missing numbers can be found by **counting back** or **counting on** from the answer.
  e.g.   20 – □ = 8
      Counting back: 20, 19, 18, 17, 16, 15 ...
      To 8 which gives the answer 12.
      Or counting on from 8 to 20, which also gives the answer 12.

Unit 30 **Subtraction to 99** page 24

1 Subtraction can be completed **horizontally** or **vertically**.
  Remember to line up units and tens in the correct columns.
  e.g. 5 tens and 2 units minus 3 tens and 1 unit can be written as
  5 – 3 tens and 2 – 1 units = 2 tens and 1 unit or 21
  e.g.

$$
\begin{array}{r} 5\,t + 2\,u \\ -\ 3\,t + 1\,u \\ \hline 2\,t + 1\,u \end{array}
\quad \text{or} \quad
\begin{array}{r} 5\,2 \\ -\ 3\,1 \\ \hline 2\,1 \end{array}
$$

2–3 See Unit 23 Nos 2–4

4 See Unit 29 No. 4

Unit 31 **Subtraction to 99 vertically** page 25

1 See Unit 23 Nos 2–4

2–3 See Unit 30 No. 1

4 Missing boxes can be found by either working out the missing subtracted numbers,
  e.g.

$$
\begin{array}{r} 2\ \Box \\ -\ 1\ 4 \\ \hline 1\ 3 \end{array}
\quad \leftarrow \quad \Box - 4 = 3 \quad \text{so} \quad \begin{array}{r} 2\ 7 \\ -\ 1\ 4 \\ \hline 1\ 3 \end{array}
$$
$$\Box = 7$$

or by working backwards and adding,
  e.g.
$$3 + 4 = \Box \qquad 7 - 4 = \Box$$
$$\Box = 7 \qquad 4 + 3 = 7$$
$$\qquad \Box = 3$$

Unit 32 **Subtracting 2 digit numbers** page 25

1 and 4 See Unit 23 Nos 2–4

2 See Unit 29 No. 2

3 The **difference between** means subtract the smaller number from the larger number (or amount).

Unit 33 **Links between addition and subtraction** page 26

1–4 Subtraction and addition are **inverse** (opposite) **operations**. This means that **subtraction** can be checked with **addition**.
  20 – 15 = 5, which can be checked by adding the answer and the subtracted number. 5 + 15 = 20
  Conversely, **addition** can be checked with **subtraction**,
  e.g. 19 + 5 = 24 and 24 – 5 = 19

Unit 34 **Multiplication as repeated addition** page 26

1 See Unit 11 No. 3

2 and 4 Addition of the **same number** (**repeated addition**) can be represented by counting the number of times the number is used to add, then multiplying this by the original number,
  e.g. in 2 + 2 + 2 + 2 the number is used 4 times.
  So 4 × 2 = 8

3 and 4 A multiplication equation can be expressed as a **repeated addition** by listing the number of times a number is added, e.g. 2 × 3 = 3 + 3 = 6

Unit 35 **Multiplication as groups** page 27

1 See Unit 11 No. 3

2–4 Multiplication is used to find the total in the number of groups or rows.
  e.g.   × × × = 6 crosses   ○ ○ = 6 circles
      × × ×   or   ○ ○
                  ○ ○

and can be expressed as 5 **groups of** 3 = 15
  e.g.

Note: **groups of** is the same as **times** or **multiplied by** or **product**.

Unit 36 **Multiplication as arrays** page 27

1 and 3 See Unit 35 Nos 2–4

2 and 4 An **array** is a set of objects generally arranged in **rows** and **columns**.
  e.g.

  4 × 3 = 12   3 × 2 = 6

It can also be found by **shading grids** to aid in the solving of an equation.

Unit 37 **Multiplication facts × 2** page 28

1 See Unit 35 Nos 2–4
2–4 See Unit 36 2 and 4

Unit 38 **Multiplication facts × 3** page 28

1 See Unit 35 Nos 2–4
2 See Unit 36 Nos 2 and 4
3 See Unit 34 Nos 3 and 4
4 See Unit 35 Nos 2–4

Unit 39 **Multiplication facts × 4** page 29

1 and 4 See Unit 35 Nos 2–4
2 See Unit 36 Nos 2 and 4
3 Multiplication equations are **reversible**,
so $2 \times 5 = 10$ and $5 \times 2 = 10$.

Unit 40 **Multiplication facts × 5** page 29

1 See Unit 35 Nos 2–4
2–3 See Unit 36 Nos 2 and 4
4 **Multiplication table grids** can be completed by multiplying
each number across by the number below the ×.

×	1	2	3
4	(1×4)	(2×4)	(3×4)
	4	8	12

Unit 41 **Multiplication facts × 6** page 30

1 See Unit 35 Nos 2–4
2 See Unit 39 No. 3
3 See Unit 36 Nos 2 and 4
4 Multiplication can be completed **horizontally** or **vertically**.
e.g. $6 \times 2 = 12$ or

$$\begin{array}{r} 6 \\ \times\ 2 \\ \hline 1\,2 \end{array}$$
Note: units and tens columns need to line up **vertically**.

Unit 42 **Multiplication facts × 7** page 30

1–3 See Unit 35 Nos 2–4
4 See Unit 41 No. 4

Unit 43 **Multiplication facts × 8** page 31

1–4. See Unit 35 Nos 2–4

Unit 44 **Multiplication facts × 9** page 31

1 See Unit 36 Nos 2 and 4
2 and 4 See Unit 35 Nos 2–4
3 Multiplication by 9 can be completed by **multiplying by 10** and
then **subtracting** the number being multiplied,
e.g.　$5 \times 9 =$
　　　$5 \times 10 = 50$
　　　subtract 5×1
　　　$50 - 5 = 45$
　　So $5 \times 9 = 45$.

Unit 45 **Multiplication facts × 10** page 32

1 See Unit 36 Nos 2 and 4
2–3 See Unit 35 Nos 2–4
4 See Unit 40 No. 4

Unit 46 **Mixed multiplication facts** page 32

1 and 3 See Unit 35 Nos 2–4
2 See Unit 41 No. 4

4 See Unit 36 Nos 2 and 4

Unit 47 **Division as sharing** page 33

1–3 **Sharing** is dividing into **equal** groups.
e.g.　6 shared between 2 is 3.

Note: sometimes there may be some left over.
e.g. 5 shared between 2, is 2 and 1 left over.
4 **One share** is the amount each person would receive if the items
were shared evenly.
e.g. 8 shared between 4 is 2. So one share is 2.

Unit 48 **Division as repeated subtraction** page 33

1–3 An amount can be **subtracted** from a number a certain
number of times to find the number of groups (**repeated
subtraction**).
e.g. $10 - 2 - 2 - 2 - 2 - 2 = 0$
　　5 groups can be made.
4 **Division** is the sharing or grouping of objects into **equal** groups.
e.g.

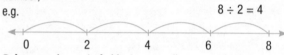

2 groups of 3
or $6 \div 2 = 3$

Divide also means how **many groups** of, or **share**.

Unit 49 **Division by 2** page 34

1 A **number line** can be used to find how many groups are in a
number,
e.g.　　　　　　　　　　　　　$8 \div 2 = 4$

```
     ___   ___   ___   ___
    /   \ /   \ /   \ /   \
<---┴-----┴-----┴-----┴-----┴--->
    0     2     4     6     8
```
2–3 An **array** is a set of objects generally arranged in **rows** and
columns. **Groups** can be circled to find how many are in a
number.
e.g.

$8 \div 4 = 2$

4 See Unit 48 No. 4

Unit 50 **Division by 3** page 34

1 See Unit 48 Nos 1–3
2 and 4 See Unit 48 No. 4
3 Multiplication and division are **inverse operations**,
e.g. $10 \times 2 = 20$ and $20 \div 2 = 10$ and $20 \div 10 = 2$

Unit 51 **Division links with multiplication facts** page 35

1–2 See Unit 50 No. 3
3 See Unit 48 No. 4
4 See Unit 36 Nos 2 and 4 and Unit 49 Nos 2–3

Unit 52 **Division with remainders** page 35

1–2 See Unit 47 Nos 1–3
3–4 When a division or grouping is made, and there are some
items or numbers left over, these are called **remainders**. The
abbreviation for remainder is r,
e.g. $10 \div 3$ asks how many groups of 3 in 10. There are 3
groups of 3 and 1 left over. This can be written as 3 r 1.

Unit 53 Rounding numbers (1)   page 36

1 **Rounding** is giving an approximate answer. For **rounding to the nearest ten**, numbers ending in the digits 0, 1, 2, 3, 4 are rounded down, and numbers ending in the digits 5, 6, 7, 8, 9 are rounded up, e.g. to the nearest ten, 142 is rounded down to 140 and 146 is rounded up to 150.

2, 3 and 4 **Rounding to the nearest hundred**, if the numbers being considered end in 01 to 49, then the number is rounded down. If the numbers being considered end in 50 to 99 the number is rounded up, e.g. to the nearest hundred, 326 is rounded down to 300 and 386 is rounded up to 400.

Unit 54 Rounding numbers (2)   page 36

1 See Unit 53 No. 1

2–3 See Unit 53 Nos 2, 3 and 4

4 When solving equations, round the numbers first and then complete the operation. This will provide an **estimated answer**.

Unit 55 Using number lines   page 37

1 See Unit 22 No. 3   2 See Unit 29 No. 2

3 A **number line** can be used to complete the multiplication equation by completing the number of jumps.

e.g. $3 \times 3 = 9$

4 See Unit 49 No. 1

Unit 56 Inverse operations   page 37

1–2 See Unit 33 Nos 1–4

3–4 See Unit 50 No. 3

Unit 57 Missing numbers   page 38

1 See Unit 13 No. 3

2 See Unit 26 No. 4

3–4 **Missing numbers** can be found by using multiplication facts, and the fact that multiplication and division are inverse operations.

Unit 58 Calculators addition and subtraction   page 38

1–3 A **calculator** can be used to find answers to equations or to check answers.

4 A **number sentence** is a written equation generally from a worded question or diagram. From here a calculator can be used to help find the answer.
Note: A word problem/story can be written for a number sentence.

Unit 59 Calculators multiplication and division   page 39

1–3 See Unit 58 Nos 1–3

4 See Unit 58 No. 4

Unit 60 Number sequences 2s and 3s   page 39

1–3 A **number sequence** is a counting pattern, which can be determined by finding the difference between pairs of numbers. This sequence is then continued, e.g. 3, 5, 7, 9
The **difference between** 3 and 5 is 2, the difference between 5 and 7 is 2. So the number sequence is counting by 2s. It is getting larger, so it is counting on.
The **next number** in the sequence is 11 as $9 + 2 = 11$

4 See Unit 6 Nos 3 and 4.

Unit 61 Number sequences 5s and 10s   page 40

1, 2 and 4 See Unit 60 Nos 1–3

3 A **rule** is an instruction that applies to a sequence of numbers or a pattern, e.g. for 3, 5, 7, 9 the rule is starting at 3 and counting on by 2.

Unit 62 Number sequences (1)   page 40

1 See Unit 60 Nos 1–3

2 See Unit 61 No. 3

3 The **tenth number** can be found by examining the sequence and completing the sequence.

4 See Unit 16 No. 4

Unit 63 Number sequences (2)   page 41

1 See Unit 6 Nos 3 and 4

2 See Unit 16 No. 4

3 See Unit 62 No. 3

4 See Unit 61 No. 3

Unit 64 Number sentences   page 41

1, 2 and 4 See Unit 58 No. 4

3 See Unit 13 No. 3, Unit 26 No. 4 and Unit 57 Nos 3–4

Unit 65 Naming fractions (1)   page 42

1–2 The **numerator** is the top number of the fraction (over the line). It shows how many parts out of the whole.
The **denominator** is the bottom number of the fraction (the number under the line). It shows how many parts there are in the whole,
e.g. $\frac{1}{3}$ is 1 out of 3 equal parts.

3–4 Fractions can be represented with **pictures** or **diagrams** where the **fraction is the shaded part**.
e.g. $\frac{1}{2}$ = or   or

Fractions can be represented with **words** or **numbers**,
e.g. one third and $\frac{1}{3}$ and

Unit 66 Naming fractions (2)   page 42

1 and 3 See Unit 65 Nos 3–4

2 and 4 Fractions can be part of a **whole** or part of a **group**.
e.g. $\frac{1}{4}$ or

Unit 67 Halves   page 43

1 and 3 **Half** is 1 out of 2 pieces. We represent a half of a shape by dividing the shape evenly into 2, and then colouring one of the pieces.
e.g.   or

2 and 4 **Half of a group** can be found by counting the total number of items in the group then dividing by 2. That number is then shaded.
e.g. or

Unit 68 Quarters
page 43

1 A **quarter** is 1 out of 4 equal pieces. We can represent a quarter by dividing the shape evenly into 4, then colouring one of the pieces.

e.g. or or

2 **3 quarters** is 3 out of 4 pieces.

e.g. or or

3–4 **A quarter of a group** can be found by counting the total number of items in the group and then dividing by 4. That number is then shaded.

e.g. or

Unit 69 Eighths
page 44

1, 2 and 4 An **eighth** is 1 out of 8 equal pieces. We can represent an eighth by dividing the shape evenly into 8, then colouring one of the pieces.

e.g. or or

3–4 An **eighth of a group** can be found by counting the total number of items in the group and then dividing by 8. The number can then be shaded.

e.g. or

Unit 70 Tenths
page 44

1–3 A **tenth** is one part of one unit which is divided evenly into 10 equal parts.

e.g.

4 A **number line** can be used to order fractions.

Unit 71 Naming fractions (3)
page 45

1–4 See Unit 65 Nos 3–4

Unit 72 Money coins
page 45

1–2 There are six different **coins** in Australia's money system: 5c, 10c, 20c, 50c, $1 and $2.

3–4 The **totals** can be found by adding the values together. Note 100 cents = $1.

Unit 73 Money notes
page 46

1 There are five different **notes** in Australia's money system: $5, $10, $20, $50 and $100.

2–3 The **totals** can be found by adding the values together.

4 To make a **total of $50**, add the amount given and then count on to $50,

e.g. + = $30, $30 + $20 = $50

Unit 74 Money
page 46

1 See Unit 72 Nos 1–2 and Unit 73 No. 1

2–4 See Unit 73 Nos 3–4 and Unit 73 Nos 2–3

Unit 75 Patterns with numbers
page 47

1 See Unit 60 Nos 1–3

2 See Unit 13 No. 3

3 A number pattern can be shown on a **number line**. For example:

counting by 5s

0   5   10   15   20

4 A number pattern can be described in **words** or with a **rule**. See Unit 61 No. 3

Unit 76 Patterns with shapes
page 47

1 The **pattern** can be completed by looking at the first part of the pattern and then repeating it.

2–4 A pattern with shapes can be described in **words** or with a **rule**. See Unit 61 No. 3

Unit 77 Solving problems (addition)
page 48

1 and 4 See Unit 11 No. 3

2 See Unit 18 No. 3

3 A **word problem** is a problem written in words. So an equation such as $1 + 3 = \square$ can be written as a story such as 1 tree plus 3 more trees equals how many trees?

Unit 78 Solving problems (subtraction)
page 48

1 and 4 See Unit 23 Nos 2–4

2 See Unit 18 No. 3

3 See Unit 77 No. 3

Unit 79 2D shapes (1)
page 49

1–3 **2D shapes** have two dimensions, length and width. They do not have depth. See Geometry Unit (page 9).

4 A shape can be described in **words**, naming the **main features** such as the number of sides and if the sides are straight.

Unit 80 2D shapes (2)
page 49

1 A **side** is one of the lines that makes a shape, or a border of a shape, e.g.

side → ← side

2 A **corner** is where sides meet,

e.g. corner corner corner

3–4 See Unit 79 Nos 1–3.

Unit 81 Squares and rectangles
page 50

1 A **square** is a 4 sided shape with 4 right angles, where all sides are the same length.

2 See Unit 79 Nos 1–3

3 See Unit 80 No. 1

4 See Unit 80 No. 2

Unit 82 Kites, rhombuses and circles
page 50

1 See Unit 79 Nos 1–3

2 See Unit 80 No. 1

3 A **rhombus** is a 'pushed over' square. It has 4 sides,

e.g.

4 See Unit 80 No. 2

Unit 83 3D Objects (1) page 51

1 See Unit 79 Nos 1–3

2 A **3D object** has height, width and length, e.g.

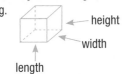

3 See Geometry Unit p. 9

4 A **surface** is the top or outside layer of an object. It can be flat or curved, e.g.

Unit 84 3D objects (2) page 51

1 A **face** is a flat surface on a 3D object. e.g.

2 See Unit 80 No. 2.

3 See Unit 80 No. 1.

4 See Unit 79 Nos 1–3

Unit 85 Length informal (1) page 52

1–2 **Length** is the distance from one end to the other or how long something is.
The **longest** object will be the object with the greatest length, when objects are compared side by side. The **shortest** object will be the object with the least length.

3–4 Objects such as a finger and a piece of string can be used to measure objects to give an estimate. e.g.

A **hand span** is the distance across a fully stretched hand.

Unit 86 Length informal (2) page 52

1–2 See Unit 85 Nos 1–2

3–4 See Unit 85 Nos 3–4

Unit 87 Comparing length page 53

1–4 See Unit 85 Nos 1–2

Unit 88 Area (1) page 53

1–4 **Area** is the size of a surface. It is measured in **square units**. It can be found by comparing informally such as counting the number of objects that cover the surface or counting squares on the shape.
e.g. Area = 6 square units

Unit 89 Area (2) page 54

1–4 See Unit 88 Nos 1–4

Unit 90 Comparing area page 54

1–4 See Unit 88 Nos 1–4

Unit 91 Capacity informal page 55

1, 2 and 4 **Capacity** is the amount a container can hold.
The object with the **greatest capacity** will be the object that can hold the most, e.g. water.

3 Smaller measuring containers e.g. measuring jugs are generally used to measure **smaller capacities**, while **larger containers** e.g. buckets are used to measure **larger capacities**.

Unit 92 Cubic centimetres page 55

1–2 A **cubic centimetre** is a standard unit used for measuring volume. The number of cubic centimetres in an object can be found by counting the number of cubes.
e.g.  there are 3 cubes

3–4 The **largest model** is the one with the most cubes. The **smallest model** is the one with the least cubes.

Unit 93 Ordering volume page 56

1 See Unit 92 Nos 1–2

2 See Unit 92 Nos 3–4

3 See Unit 91 Nos 1, 2 and 4. Note: the amounts can be read off the sides of the containers.

Unit 94 Mass informal (1) page 56

1 and 4 **Mass** is the amount of matter in an object. **Heavier objects** will be lower on the scales, while **lighter objects** will be higher on the scales.
e.g.

heavier object   lighter object

2 The **heaviest object** is the one that would take the most effort to pick up.

3 To **balance the scales** the same number (or equal mass) should be on each side of the scales.
e.g.

Unit 95 Mass informal (2) page 57

1–2 See Unit 94 No. 2

3–4 See Unit 94 No. 3

Unit 96 Time analogue (hour) page 57

1–3 **Time** is the space between one event and the next. It is measured on a **clock**. An **analogue clock** uses the numerals 1 to 12 and rotating hands to show the time. On the **hour**, the long hand points to the 12 and is read as **o'clock** (according to the number the small hand points to),
e.g.

3 o'clock

4 Time that has a **smaller number** of the hour position will occur earlier in the day.

Unit 97 Time analogue (half hour) page 58

1–3 On the **half hour**, the long hand is pointing to the 6, and is read as **half past**. The short hand is pointing to half way between the hours,
e.g.

half past 7

4 See Unit 96 No. 4

Unit 98 **Time analogue (quarter past)** page 58

1–4 On the **quarter hour**, the long hand is pointing to the 3, and is read as **quarter past**. The hour hand is slightly past the hour, e.g.

 quarter past 5

Unit 99 **Time analogue (quarter to)** page 59

1 There are **60 minutes in one hour, 30 minutes in half an hour, 15 minutes in a quarter of an hour**.

2–4 On the **three-quarter hour**, the long hand is pointing to the 9 is read as **quarter to**. The hour hand is pointing almost to the next hour, e.g.

 quarter to 9

Unit 100 **Digital time (1)** page 59

1–3 A **digital clock** only uses numerals to show the time. This can be expressed in **words** e.g. seven forty-five is 7:45. The numbers after the dots mean minutes past, e.g. 1:15 means 15 minutes past 1.

4 The link can be shown between **digital and analogue** clocks/time, as :00 means o'clock, :30 means half past, :15 means a quarter past and :45 means a quarter to. Note a quarter to is to the next o'clock time, e.g. 3:45 is a quarter to 4.

3:45

Unit 101 **Digital time (2)** page 60

1–3 See Unit 100 No. 4.
4 See Unit 100 Nos 1–3.

Unit 102 **Months** page 60

1–3 There are 12 **months** in a year. January, February, March, April, May, June, July, August, September, October, November and December. On a typical Australian calendar January is the first month and December the last.

4 Month names can be **abbreviated** (shortened), e.g. Jan = January and Feb = February.

Unit 103 **Seasons** page 61

1 There are 4 **seasons**: Summer, Autumn, Winter and Spring.

2–4 In most of Australia, **Summer** is December, January, February. **Autumn** is March, April, May. **Winter** is June, July, August. **Spring** is September, October, November.

Unit 104 **Calendars** page 61

1 and 3 There are 12 **months** in a year, 7 **days** in a week, 14 days in a **fortnight**. 31 days in January, March, May, July, August, October and December. February has 28/29 days and the rest 30.

2 The **days of the week** are Monday, Tuesday, Wednesday, Thursday, Friday, Saturday and Sunday.

4 The **date** is the number of the day of the month, i.e. the 4th day of September is September 4.

Unit 105 **Position** page 62

1–4 The **position** of an object is its place in relation to the things around it. It can be defined by using terms such as **left/right** or **up/down**.

x	y	z
A	B	C

i.e. C is to the right of B.

Unit 106 **Position – giving directions** page 62

1–3 Terms such as **next to**, **between** and **near** can also be used to describe something's **position**. Also see Unit 105 Nos 1–4

4 A **grid** can be used to give directions, e.g. 2 squares up and 3 squares to the right.

Unit 107 **Maps** page 63

1–2 A **grid reference** is used to show position on a grid. It is represented by pairs of letters or numbers, e.g. A2.

3–4 A **map** is a diagram of a place that shows its position in the area or the world. See also Unit 105 Nos 1–4

Unit 108 **Transformations (slide)** page 63

1–4 A **slide** describes the movement of an object from one place to another without a change in its shape. e.g.

Unit 109 **Transformations (flip)** page 64

1–4 A **flip** describes the movement of an object across a line to face the other direction, making a mirror image. e.g.

Unit 110 **Transformations (quarter turn)** page 64

1–4 A **turn** describes the movement of an object rotating about a point. A quarter turn describes a turn equal to a quarter of a circle (or 90 degrees). The object can be turned left or right. e.g.

Unit 111 **Transformations (half turn)** page 65

1–4 See Unit 110 Nos 1–4. Note: a half turn is where the object has been moved half a circle (or 180 degrees). e.g.

Unit 112 **Angles** page 65

1–4 An **angle** is the amount of turn between two straight lines (arms) fixed at a point.

Note: is larger than

A **right angle** is indicated by:
It is equal to 90 degrees.

Unit 113 Chance
page 66

1, 2 and 4 Chance is the probability or likelihood of something happening. It can be described with words such as certain, likely, unlikely, impossible or equal chance.

3 Outcomes are the number of different options possible for an event.

Unit 114 Organising data
page 66

1–3 Tables can be used to collect data in rows and columns.

e.g.

Heads	5
Tails	6

Colour	Number
Red	6
Green	5
Blue	10

A **tally** uses marks to record counting.

| = 1, || = 2, ||| = 3, |||| = 4, ⊦⊦⊦ = 5, ⊦⊦⊦ ⊦⊦⊦ = 10

4 Information from tables can be read to answer questions.

Unit 115 Picture graphs
page 67

1–4 A **picture graph** is a graph which uses pictures to represent amounts,
e.g.

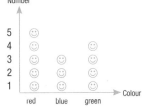

Note: **least** common/popular things have the **lowest** number of pictures and the **most** popular have the **highest** number of pictures.

Unit 116 Reading data
page 67

1 and 3 See Unit 114 Nos 1–3

2 A **tick sheet** is another way of tallying information,
e.g.

cat	✓ ✓ ✓ ✓
dog	✓ ✓ ✓ ✓ ✓ ✓

4 See Unit 115 Nos 1–4

Unit 117 Addition practice
page 68

1 See Unit 11 No. 1 and No. 3
2 See Unit 20 Nos 2–3
3–4 See Unit 11 No. 3

Unit 118 Subtraction practice
page 68

1 See Unit 24 No. 4
2 See Unit 23 Nos 2–4
3 See Unit 30 No. 1
4 See Unit 31 No. 4

Unit 119 Multiplication practice
page 69

1 See Unit 34 Nos 2 and 4, Unit 35 Nos 2–4 and Unit 36 Nos 2–4
2 See Unit 35 Nos 2–4
3 See Unit 41 No. 4
4 See Unit 40 No. 4

Unit 120 Division practice
page 69

1 and 3 See Unit 48 No. 4
2 See Unit 50 No. 3
4 See Unit 52 Nos 3–4

Geometry Unit

2-dimensional shapes

 square

 rectangle

 rhombus

 kite

 triangle

circle

3-dimensional shapes

 sphere

 cone

 cylinder

 cube

 rectangular prism

 triangular prism

 square pyramid

 triangular pyramid

Numbers to 100

1 Write the **number** shown by the Base ten blocks:

a _____

b _____

c _____

d _____

2 Write the **number** shown by the Unifix (linking) blocks:

a _____

b _____

c _____

_____

3 Write each as a **numeral**:

a nineteen _____

b sixty-five _____

c thirty-seven _____

d fifty _____

4 Write each of the following in **words**:

a 11 _____

b 48 _____

c 53 _____

d 99 _____

5 Write the **number** shown by the Base ten blocks:

_____

6 Write the **number** shown by the Unifix (linking) blocks:

_____

7 Write seventy-three as a **numeral**. _____

8 Write 14 in **words**. _____

9 Circle the **larger number**:   Fifty-three or 15

Place value

1 What is the **value** of the 2 in each of the following numbers?

a 27 _____

b 52 _____

c 12 _____

d 2 _____

2 Circle the **larger number** in each pair:

a 19 or 91

b 53 or 35

c 40 or 4

d 98 or 89

3 Write the **number** shown by the bundling sticks:

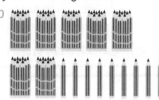

a _____

b _____

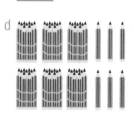

c _____

d _____

_____

4 Write the **next number** after:

a 49 _____

b 76 _____

c 81 _____

d 30 _____

5 What is the **value** of the 2 in 82? _____

6 Circle the **larger number**:   75 or 57

7 Write the **number** shown by the bundling sticks:

_____

8 Write the **next number** after 19. _____

9 Write the next number after 57 in **words**.

_____

Numbers to 1000

1 Write the **number** shown on the abacus:

a

_____

b

_____

c

_____

d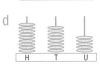

_____

2 How many **digits** are in each of the following numbers?

a 237 _____   b 104 _____

c 19 _____   d 500 _____

3 Write in **words**:

a 852 _____

b 917 _____

c 105 _____

d 400 _____

4 Write as a **numeral**:

a three hundred and eleven _____

b six hundred and forty _____

c seven hundred and three _____

d nine hundred and fifty eight _____

5 Write the **number** shown on the abacus:

_____

6 How many **digits** are in 920? _____

7 Write 390 in **words**. _____

8 Write eight hundred and seventy-six as a **numeral**.

_____

9 Write the **numeral** for:
3 hundreds 8 tens 6 units _____

Ordering numbers (1)

1 What is the **digit** in the tens place in each of the following numbers?

a 496 _____   b 235 _____

c 111 _____   d 608 _____

2 Order the numbers from **smallest to largest**:

a 49, 85, 76, 53 _____

b 140, 114, 124, 134 _____

c 856, 327, 475, 682 _____

d 507, 209, 403, 105 _____

3 Order the numbers from **largest to smallest**:

a 56, 65, 6, 57 _____

b 420, 520, 321, 48 _____

c 861, 875, 900, 883 _____

d 103, 301, 130, 310 _____

4 What is the **next number after** the one given?

a 99 _____   b 104 _____

c 300 _____   d 865 _____

5 What is the **digit** in the tens place in 421?

_____

6 Order the numbers from **smallest to largest**:
529, 580, 566, 520

_____

7 Order the numbers from **largest to smallest**:
809, 908, 918, 890

_____

8 What is the **next number after** 777?

_____

9 True or false? 210 is **larger** than 201.

_____

Ordering numbers (2)

1 Write the **smallest** possible **number** using all of the digits:

a 4, 2, 3 _____

b 9, 7, 8 _____

c 4, 0, 1 _____

d 3, 7, 5 _____

2 Write the **largest** possible **number** using all of the digits:

a 7, 8, 6 _____

b 9, 3, 5 _____

c 4, 7, 5 _____

d 8, 9, 0 _____

3 Arrange the numbers from **smallest to largest**:

a 98, 75, 89, 57 _____

b 101, 97, 115, 108 _____

c 527, 896, 666, 785 _____

d 321, 123, 231, 312 _____

4 Circle the **largest number** in each pair:

a 96 or 69

b 107 or 170

c 153 or 351

d 111 or 101

5 Write the **smallest** possible **number** using 1, 6, 3.

_____

6 Write the **largest** possible **number** using 2, 3, 1.

_____

7 Arrange the numbers from **smallest to largest**:
426, 624, 428, 604

_____

8 Circle the **larger number**: 476 or 764

9 **True or false?** 989 is **less than** 998. _____

Counting forwards and backwards

1 Write the **number after**:

a 206 _____

b 785 _____

c 396 _____

d 428 _____

2 Write the **number before**:

a 729 _____

b 856 _____

c 407 _____

d 290 _____

3 **Start** at:

a 35 and **count forwards** by 3 _____

b 35 and **count forwards** by 7 _____

c 35 and **count forwards** by 11 _____

d 35 and **count forwards** by 20 _____

4 **Start** at:

a 49 and **count backwards** by 5 _____

b 49 and **count backwards** by 9 _____

c 49 and **count backwards** by 11 _____

d 49 and **count backwards** by 20 _____

5 Write the next **number after** 910. _____

6 Write the **number before** 336. _____

7 **Start** at 35 and **count forwards** by 9. _____

8 **Start** at 49 and **count backwards** by 3. _____

9 If I **start** at 100, how many do I need to go **forwards** to stop at 113?

_____

Expanding 2-digit numbers

1 Use the **number expander** to expand the following numbers:

a 37 | T | U |

b 56 | T | U |

c 72 | T | U |

d 90 | T | U |

2 Write the **numeral** for:

a 20 + 6 _____

b 40 + 3 _____

c 90 + 1 _____

d 70 + 9 _____

3 **Expand**:

a 17 _____

b 66 _____

c 84 _____

d 97 _____

4 Write the **value** of each of the underlined digits:

a 6̲2 _____ b 2̲9 _____

c 4̲1 _____ d 6̲0̲ _____

5 Use the **number expander** to expand 17:

| T | U |

6 Write 60 + 4 as a **numeral**. _____

7 **Expand** 35. _____

8 Write the **value** of the underlined digit in 1̲5.

_____

9 Draw a **picture** to represent 73.

Expanding 3-digit numbers

1 Write the **number** shown on each abacus:

a   b

_____   _____

c   d

_____   _____

2 Write the **numeral**:

a 600 + 20 + 5 _____

b 900 + 70 + 1 _____

c 400 + 30 + 9 _____

d 800 + 6 _____

3 **Expand**:

a 157 _____

b 708 _____

c 555 _____

d 220 _____

4 Write the **digit** in the tens position in each of the numbers:

a 437 _____

b 117 _____

c 856 _____

d 330 _____

5 Write the **number** shown on the abacus:

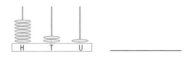   _____

6 Write 300 + 60 + 3 as a **numeral**. _____

7 **Expand** 811. _____

8 What is the **digit** in the tens position of 906?

_____

9 Write in words the **largest number** possible using all of the digits: 5, 7, 3.

_____

Expanding 4-digit numbers

1 Write the following **numbers** as shown on the number expanders:

a | 8 | Th | 4 | H | 7 | T | 6 | U | _____

b | 3 | Th | 7 | H | 9 | T | 1 | U | _____

c | 2 | Th | 2 | H | 4 | T | 6 | U | _____

d | 1 | Th | 1 | H | 9 | T | 5 | U | _____

2 Write the **value** of each of the underlined digits:

a 372<u>1</u> _____ b 5<u>8</u>06 _____

c <u>7</u>200 _____ d 41<u>99</u> _____

3 Write the **numeral**:

a 6000 + 300 + 20 + 5 _____

b 1000 + 400 _____

c 7000 + 700 + 5 _____

d 9000 + 800 + 50 + 1 _____

4 **Expand**:

a 6666 _____

b 1507 _____

c 9795 _____

d 5901 _____

5 Write the **number** as shown on the number expander:

| 6 | Th | 2 | H | 9 | T | 8 | U | _____

6 Write the **value** of the underlined digit in 13<u>9</u>6.

_____

7 Write 2000 + 400 + 60 as a **numeral**.

_____

8 **Expand** 3350. _____

9 Draw an **abacus** to show the **number** 7521.

Ordering numbers (3)

1 Write the **largest** possible **number** with all of the given digits:

a 7, 8, 6, 3 _____

b 2, 1, 0, 9 _____

c 4, 4, 8, 5 _____

d 7, 5, 3, 4 _____

2 Write the **smallest** possible **number** with all of the given digits:

a 2, 1, 8, 3 _____

b 7, 9, 4, 2 _____

c 4, 1, 9, 7 _____

d 1, 8, 3, 4 _____

3 Circle the **smaller number** in each pair:

a 96 or 79

b 147 or 471

c 2785 or 7285

d 3851 or 3840

4 Arrange each set of numbers from **smallest to largest**:

a 58, 76, 30, 47 _____

b 109, 170, 185, 156 _____

c 1146, 1785, 1432, 1298 _____

d 7856, 7896, 7736, 7046 _____

5 Write the **largest** possible **number** using 4, 6, 1, 8.

_____

6 Write the **smallest** possible **number** using 3, 6, 7, 1.

_____

7 Circle the **smaller number** in 4329 or 6385.

8 Arrange 5893, 4782, 6115, 8908 from **smallest to largest**.

_____

9 Write all of the **different combinations** of 3 digit numbers using 8, 7, 6.

_____

Simple addition

1 Find the **totals** on the tens frames:

a

_____

b

_____

c

_____

d

_____

2 Find the **totals** of the Unifix blocks:

a +   _____

b   +   _____

c   +   _____

d   +   _____

3 **Complete**:

a 4 + 2 = _____   b 3 + 5 = _____

c 7 + 1 = _____   d 1 + 4 = _____

4 Use the **open number lines** to solve the addition number sentences:

a 5 + 4 = _____

b 6 + 2 = _____

c 8 + 4 = _____

d 9 + 6 = _____

5 Find the **total** on the tens frames:

_____

6 Find the **total** of the Unifix blocks:

 +   _____

7 **Complete**: 5 + 4 = _____

8 Use the **open number line** to find: 7 + 5 = _____

9 Find the **total** of the tens frames: _____

Counting on

1 **Count on** to complete:

a 7 + 5 = _____   b 6 + 5 = _____

c 9 + 5 = _____   d 8 + 5 = _____

2 Start at:

a 15 and **count on** by 3 _____

b 15 and **count on** by 7 _____

c 15 and **count on** by 8 _____

d 15 and **count on** by 6 _____

3 Start at 27 and:

a **count on** by 3 _____

b and now **count on** by 7 _____

c and now **count on** by 8 _____

d and now **count on** by 10 _____

4 Complete the **open number lines** to show the number sentences and the answers:

a 8 + 4 = _____

b 6 + 7 = _____

c 9 + 6 = _____

d 5 + 7 = _____

5 **Count on** by 5 to complete: 11 + 5 = _____

6 Start at 15 and **count on** by 9. _____

7 Start at 27 and **count on** by 6. _____

8 Complete the **open number line** to find:

8 + 7 = _____

9 I start at 27. How many do I need to **count on** to reach 50?

_____

Building to 10

1 Find the number of counters missing on the tens frames to **make 10**.

a _____

b _____

c _____

d _____

2 Find how many more blocks are needed to **make 10**. Write a number sentence.

a ☐ + ☐ = 10

b ☐ + ☐ = 10

c ☐ + ☐ = 10

d ☐ + ☐ = 10

3 **Complete** the number sentences:

a $2 + $ ___ $= 10$ b $6 + $ ___ $= 10$

c $9 + $ ___ $= 10$ d $10 + $ ___ $= 10$

4 Circle the numbers that **add to 10** and then complete the answers:

a $4 + 2 + 6 = $ ___   b $8 + 2 + 4 = $ ___

c $9 + 1 + 5 = $ ___   d $5 + 3 + 7 = $ ___

5 Find the number of counters missing on the tens frame to **make 10**:

 _____

6 Find how many more blocks are needed to **make 10**. Write a number sentence.

☐ + ☐ = 10

7 **Complete**: $4 + $ ___ $= 10$

8 Circle the numbers that **add to 10** and then complete the answer: $5 + 6 + 4 = $ _____

9 Circle the numbers that **add to 100** and then complete the equation: $60 + 70 + 40 = $ _____

Doubles

1 **Double** by drawing the same number of counters on the tens frames and then count all to find the total:

a + [ ] = _____

b + [ ] = _____

c + [ ] = _____

d + [ ] = _____

2 **Double** by drawing the same number of blocks and then **count on** to find the total.

a +   = _____

b +   = _____

c +   = _____

d +   = _____

3 Circle the number which is the **double** to complete the number sentence:

a $4 + $ ___ $= 8$ (4, 5, 6)   b $6 + $ ___ $= 12$ (4, 5, 6)

c $5 + $ ___ $= 10$ (4, 5, 6)   d $7 + $ ___ $= 14$ (5, 6, 7)

4 Complete the **additions**:

a $2 + 2 = $ _____   b $9 + 9 = $ _____

c $10 + 10 = $ _____   d $3 + 3 = $ _____

5 **Double** by drawing the same number of counters on the tens frames and then count all to find the total:

+ [ ] = _____

6 **Double** by drawing the same number of blocks and then **count on** to find the total.

+   = _____

7 Circle the number which is the **double** to complete the equation:

$8 + 7, 8, 9 = 16$

8 **Complete**: $7 + 7 = $ _____

9 Find the **doubles** of:

a 12 _____   b 15 _____   c 20 _____

Tens facts

1 Complete the **additions**:

a 1 + 2 = _____

   10 + 20 = _____

b 2 + 3 = _____

   20 + 30 = _____

c 5 + 3 = _____

   50 + 30 = _____

d 6 + 3 = _____

   60 + 30 = _____

2 Complete the **doubles**:

a 10 + 10 = _____

b 30 + 30 = _____

c 40 + 40 = _____

d 20 + 20 = _____

3 Build to the **nearest 10**:

a 22 + _____ = 30

b 15 + _____ = 20

c 47 + _____ = 50

d 64 + _____ = 70

4 Circle the numbers that **build to 100** and then complete the addition:

a 40 + 60 + 20 = _____

b 80 + 20 + 10 = _____

c 40 + 70 + 30 = _____

d 20 + 50 + 50 = _____

5 **Complete**:

5 + 4 = _____

50 + 40 = _____

6 Complete the **double**:

50 + 50 = _____

7 Build to the **nearest 10**:

33 + _____ = 40

8 Circle the numbers that **build to 100** and complete the addition:

50 + 30 + 70 = _____

9 Tony had 3 blocks, Veronica 5 blocks and Damon 7. How many blocks were there **altogether**?

Adding 10

1 **Complete** the addition by adding 10:

a + ☐ + ☐ = _____

b ☐ + ☐ = _____

c 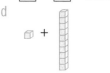 ☐ + ☐ = _____

d ☐ + ☐ = _____

2 **Complete**:

a 5 + 10 = _____

b 9 + 10 = _____

c 8 + 10 = _____

d 2 + 10 = _____

3 **Count on** by 10:

a from 16 = _____

b from 19 = _____

c from 21 = _____

d from 35 = _____

4 **Complete**:

a

+	1	2	3	4
10				

b

+	7	8	9	10
10				

c

+	5	6	7	8
10				

d

+	11	12	13	14
10				

5 **Complete** the addition by adding 10:

 + 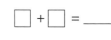 ☐ + ☐ = _____

6 **Complete**: 6 + 10 = _____

7 **Count on** 10 from 12. _____

8 **Complete**:

+	25	26	27	28
10				

9 Complete to find the **original numbers**:

+					
10	29	17	36	42	

Commutative law

1 Complete the **additions**:

a 2 + 3 = _____   b 7 + 1 = _____

   3 + 2 = _____   1 + 7 = _____

c 4 + 5 = _____   d 6 + 3 = _____

   5 + 4 = _____   3 + 6 = _____

2 Complete the **missing numbers**:

a 2 + 7 = 7 + _____   b 6 + 1 = 1 + _____

c 3 + 4 = 4 + _____   d 5 + 2 = 2 + _____

3 Match the **number sentences** that are equal:

a 5 + 2   5 + 4

b 3 + 0   7 + 1

c 4 + 5   2 + 5

d 1 + 7   0 + 3

4 Complete the **missing numbers**:

a 6 + _____ = 8 = 2 + _____

b 5 + _____ = 6 = 1 + _____

c _____ + 2 = 9 = _____ + 7

d _____ + 1 = 5 = _____ + 4

5 **Complete:**   5 + 2 = _____
                   2 + 5 = _____

6 **Complete:**   6 + 3 = 3 + _____

7 Circle the **number sentence** with the same answer as: 2 + 5

5 + 2   7 + 1   3 + 6

8 Complete the **missing numbers**:

9 + _____ = 9 = 0 + _____

9 Complete the **open number line** for the following two number sentences:

6 + 2 = _____   ⟵————————⟶

2 + 6 = _____   ⟵————————⟶

What do you notice?

_____

_____

Adding to 20

1 **Complete:**

a    b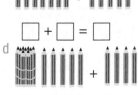

☐ + ☐ = ☐   ☐ + ☐ = ☐

c 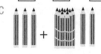   d

☐ + ☐ = ☐   ☐ + ☐ = ☐

2 **Complete:**

a 8 + 11 = _____   b 7 + 5 = _____

c 10 + 6 = _____   d 6 + 8 = _____

3 Write the **number sentence** and find the **answer** to:

a six plus two equals _____

b nine plus four equals _____

c seven plus twelve equals _____

d four plus thirteen equals _____

4 Find the **correct answers** from the answer bank:

15, 12, 18, 16, 17, 19

a 8 + 10 = _____   b 6 + 9 = _____

c 4 + 8 = _____   d 13 + 4 = _____

5 **Complete:**

   _____ + _____ = _____

6 **Complete:** 7 + 7 = _____

7 Write the **number sentence** and **answer** to:

eleven plus seven equals _____

8 Find the **correct answer** from the answer bank:

16, 20, 15, 14, 12

8 + 8 = _____

9 Find the **answer** for:

3 + 2 + 7 + 5 = _____

Explain how you did it.

_____

_____

Adding to 50

1 Write and solve the **number sentence** for:

a 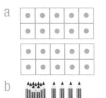 + = _____

b  + = _____

c   + = _____

d 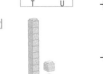 + = _____

2 Complete:

a 12 + 15 = ____   b 40 + 9 = ____
c 17 + 22 = ____   d 15 + 11 = ____

3 Complete:

a

+	1	11	21	31
5				

b

+	12	22	32	42
3				

c

+	4	14	24	34
4				

d

+	6	16	26	36
10				

4 Find the **missing numbers**:

a 20 + ☐ = 30   b 12 + ☐ = 25
c 15 + ☐ = 27   d 15 + ☐ = 36

5 Write and solve the **number sentence** for:

 + = _____

6 Complete: 14 + 14 = _____

7 Complete:

+	15	25	35	45
2				

8 Find the **missing number**: 17 + ☐ = 39

9 Draw a **picture** to show the number sentence and solve it: 15 + 14 = ____

Adding to 99

1 Write and solve the **number sentence** for:

a  = _____

b 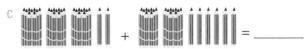 = _____

c  = _____

d + = _____

2 Complete:

a 4 tens and 6 units + 3 tens and 2 units = _____
b 5 tens and 2 units + 4 tens and 1 unit = _____
c 6 tens and 2 units + 2 tens and 7 units = _____
d 8 tens and 3 units + 1 ten and 2 units = _____

3 Find:

a 50 + 25 = _____   b 38 + 11 = _____
c 84 + 14 = _____   d 26 + 32 = _____

4 Solve the number sentence to find the **total number** altogether.

a 15 pencils and 23 pencils = _____
b 23 books and 61 books = _____
c 32 buttons and 47 buttons = _____
d 43 balls and 25 balls = _____

5 Write and solve the **number sentence** for:

= _____

6 Complete:

5 tens and 3 units + 4 tens and 6 units = _____

7 Find: 61 + 15 = _____

8 Solve the number sentence to find the **total number** of trees altogether:

22 trees and 36 trees = _____

9 Select from the following numbers and write **2 number sentences** that equal 58:

23, 41, 30, 25, 35, 17   _____

_____

Adding to 99 – vertically

1 Solve:

a $31 + 14 =$ _____   b $28 + 41 =$ _____

c $70 + 19 =$ _____   d $43 + 50 =$ _____

2 **Complete** the following:

a $\begin{array}{r} 8\,t + 2\,u \\ + 1\,t + 5\,u \\ \hline \end{array}$ b $\begin{array}{r} 5\,t + 3\,u \\ + 2\,t + 6\,u \\ \hline \end{array}$

c $\begin{array}{r} 2\,t + 5\,u \\ + 7\,t + 1\,u \\ \hline \end{array}$ d $\begin{array}{r} 3\,t + 2\,u \\ + 4\,t + 4\,u \\ \hline \end{array}$

3 Complete:

a
T	U
3	0
+ 2	1

b
T	U
2	7
+ 4	2

c
T	U
7	2
+ 1	7

d
T	U
5	6
+ 2	2

4 Find the **missing digits**:

a $\begin{array}{r} 7\ \ 2 \\ + 1\ \square \\ \hline \square\ \ 6 \end{array}$ b $\begin{array}{r} 5\ \ 0 \\ + 2\ \square \\ \hline \square\ \ 8 \end{array}$

c $\begin{array}{r} \square\ \ 5 \\ + 3\ \square \\ \hline 5\ \ 8 \end{array}$ d $\begin{array}{r} \square\ \square \\ + 4\ \ 4 \\ \hline 8\ \ 8 \end{array}$

5 **Solve**: $27 + 32 =$ _____

6 Complete: $\begin{array}{r} 5\,t + 3\,u \\ + 2\,t + 4\,u \\ \hline \end{array}$

7 Complete:
T	U
2	6
+ 5	1

8 Find the **missing digits**: $\begin{array}{r} 2\ \square \\ + \square\ \ 6 \\ \hline 6\ \ 7 \end{array}$

9 In the classroom there are 14 boys, 12 girls and the teacher. **How many** people are in the classroom?

_____

Adding 2-digit numbers

1 Find:

a $32 + 46 =$ _____

b $42 + 52 =$ _____

c $23 + 46 =$ _____

d $19 + 20 =$ _____

2 Find the **total** of:

a 23 hats and 45 hats _____

b 40 scarves and 17 scarves _____

c 62 shoes and 14 shoes _____

d 22 gloves and 60 gloves _____

3 Complete, using the **jump strategy**:

a $53 + 19 =$ _____

b $44 + 37 =$ _____

c $35 + 39 =$ _____

d $28 + 48 =$ _____

4 Complete using **groups of 20**:

a $17 + 16 + 3 =$ _____

b $5 + 17 + 15 =$ _____

c $16 + 13 + 4 =$ _____

d $12 + 8 + 26 =$ _____

5 **Find**: $17 + 52 =$ _____

6 Find the **total** of 15 sunglasses and 72 sunglasses.

_____

7 Complete using the **jump strategy**.

$17 + 56 =$ _____

8 **Complete**: $1 + 26 + 19 =$ _____

9 Draw **a number line** to show the addition and find the **answer** to:

$52 + 23 + 8 =$ _____

Simple subtraction

1 Write a **number sentence** for each of the following pictures:

a   _____

b   _____

c   _____

d   _____

2 Use the number line to help find the **differences**:

```
0        5        10       15       20
```

a   16 − 7 = ____   b   14 − 7 = ____

c   12 − 9 = ____   d   19 − 12 = ____

3 **Complete**:

a   10 **take away** 4 = _____

b   8 **minus** 5 = _____

c   **subtract** 6 from 9 = _____

d   find the **difference** between 5 and 3 = _____

4 Find how many are **left**:

a   there are 19 biscuits, 12 were eaten _____

b   there are 10 crayons, 3 broke _____

c   there were 20 chocolates, 15 were eaten _____

d   there were 12 books, 6 were borrowed _____

5 Write a **number sentence** for:

   _____

6 Find the **difference between** 13 and 7:

7 **Subtract** 4 from 6. _____

8 There were 9 balls 5 were sold. How many are **left**?

_____

9 Draw a **picture** to help solve: 20 − 14 = _____

Counting back

1 **Count back** by 3 to complete:

a   6 − 3 = _____

b   9 − 3 = _____

c   11 − 3 = _____

d   17 − 3 = _____

2 Start at:

a   30 and **count back** by 3 _____

b   30 and **count back** by 7 _____

c   30 and **count back** by 10 _____

d   30 and **count back** by 12 _____

3 Start at 27 and

a   **count back** by 5 _____

b   now **count back** by 2 _____

c   now **count back** by 10 _____

d   now **count back** by 3 _____

4 Complete the **open number lines** to show the number sentences and **answers**:

a   8 − 3 = _____

b   11 − 7 = _____

c   19 − 12 = _____

d   15 − 8 = _____

5 **Count back**: 14 − 3 = _____

6 Start at 30 and **count back** by 15 _____

7 Start at 27 and **count back** by 11 _____

8 Complete the **open number line** to show the number sentence and the **answer** to:

13 − 5 = _____

9 If I start at 40, how many do I need to **count back** to reach 22?

_____

Subtraction patterns

1 **Complete** the pattern by crossing off:

a 11 − 2 = _____	b 11 − 3 = _____
c 11 − 4 = _____	d 11 − 5 = _____
e 11 − 6 = _____	f 11 − _____ = 4
g 11 − _____ = 3	h 11 − _____ = 2

2 **Complete** the patterns:

a 9 − 4 = 5	b 7 − 3 = _____
19 − 4 = _____	17 − 3 = _____
29 − 4 = _____	27 − 3 = _____
c 8 − 5 = _____	d 9 − 6 = _____
18 − 5 = _____	19 − 6 = _____
28 − 5 = _____	29 − 6 = _____

3 **Complete**:

a 6 − 2 = _____	6 − 4 = _____
b 7 − 3 = _____	7 − 4 = _____
c 8 − 2 = _____	8 − 6 = _____
d 10 − 7 = _____	10 − 3 = _____
e 9 − 3 = _____	9 − 6 = _____
f 8 − 3 = _____	8 − 5 = _____

4 **Complete**:

a 26 − 4 = 22	b 29 − 5 = 24
26 − 14 = _____	29 − 15 = _____
26 − 24 = _____	29 − 25 = _____
c 25 − 3 = _____	d 28 − 6 = _____
25 − 13 = _____	28 − 16 = _____
25 − 23 = _____	28 − 26 = _____

5 **Complete** the pattern:

☆☆☆☆☆☆☆☆☆☆

a 12 − 4 = _____	b 12 − 5 = _____
c 12 − 6 = _____	d 12 − 7 = _____

6 **Complete** the pattern:

6 − 5 = _____   16 − 5 = _____   26 − 5 = _____

7 **Complete**:

10 − 6 = _____   10 − 4 = _____

8 **Complete**:

29 − 3 = _____   29 − 13 = _____   29 − 23 = _____

9 Write four **subtraction number sentences** which result in 4 as the answer.

_____ _____

_____ _____

10s facts

1 Use the tens frames to find the **difference**:

a   10 − ☐ = 7

b   10 − ☐ = 9

c   10 − ☐ = 3

d   10 − ☐ = 5

2 How **many more** blocks are needed to make 10? Write as a **subtraction number sentence**.

a   10 − ☐ = 4

b   10 − ☐ = 6

c   10 − ☐ = 8

d   10 − ☐ = 10

3 Complete the following **number sentences**:

a 10 − 1 = _____	b 10 − 6 = _____
c 10 − 8 = _____	d 10 − 5 = _____

4 Complete the **subtractions**:

a 11 − _____ = 10	b 15 − _____ = 10
c 18 − _____ = 10	d 13 − _____ = 10

5 Use the tens frame to find the **difference**:

10 − ☐ = 6

6 How **many more** blocks are needed to make 10? Write as a **subtraction number sentence**.

10 − ☐ = 7

7 **Complete**: 10 − 0 = _____

8 **Complete**: 14 − _____ = 10

9 **Complete** the wheel:

(wheel with centre 10−, numbers: 7 0 1 2 3 4 5 6)

Subtracting 10

1 Write a **number sentence** subtracting 1 ten:

a

$33 - 10 =$ ☐

b

_____

c

_____

d

_____

2 **Complete**:

a $21 - 10 =$ _____   b $46 - 10 =$ _____
c $35 - 10 =$ _____   d $57 - 10 =$ _____

3 Complete the **open number lines** to subtract groups of 10:

a $82 - 30 =$ ____

b $56 - 40 =$ ____

c $95 - 60 =$ ____

d $73 - 40 =$ ____

4 **Complete**:

a

–	21	31	41	51
10				

b

–	18	28	38	48
10				

c

–	47	57	67	77
10				

d

–	63	73	83	93
10				

5 Write a number sentence **subtracting 1 ten**:

_____

6 **Complete**: $38 - 10 =$ _____

7 Complete the **open number line** to subtract:

$47 - 20 =$ _____

8 **Complete**:

–	59	69	79	89
10				

9 Write as many different **subtraction number sentences** as possible using the numbers 32, 52 and 20.

_____

_____

Subtraction to 20

1 **Complete**:

a $20 - 15 =$ _____

b $17 - 6 =$ _____

c $18 - 12 =$ _____

d $14 - 3 =$ _____

2 **Answer**:

a the **difference between** 16 and 8 _____

b 19 **minus** 9 _____

c 18 **take away** 11 _____

d **subtract** 7 from 13 _____

3 Use **open number lines** to complete:

a $15 - 9 =$ _____

b $17 - 6 =$ _____

c $19 - 16 =$ ____

d $13 - 8 =$ _____

4 Complete the **pairs of number sentences**:

a $13 - 5 =$ _____ $13 - 8 =$ _____
b $11 - 6 =$ _____ $11 - 5 =$ _____
c $17 - 15 =$ _____ $17 - 2 =$ _____
d $15 - 6 =$ _____ $15 - 9 =$ _____

5 **Complete**: $14 - 9 =$ _____

6 Find 17 **take away** $10 =$ _____

7 Use the **open number line** to complete:

$15 - 11 =$ _____

8 Complete the **pair of number sentences**:

$12 - 7 =$ _____ $12 - 5 =$ _____

9 Complete the **missing numbers**:

$8 + 7 =$ ☐

☐ $- 8 = 7$

☐ $- 7 = 8$

Subtraction to 50

1   **Complete**:

   a $35 - 8 = $ _____

   b $27 - 6 = $ _____

   c $45 - 9 = $ _____

   d $14 - 8 = $ _____

2   Use the **jump strategy** to complete:

   a $30 - 12$ think $30 - 10 - 2 = $ _____

   b $47 - 22$ think $47 - 20 - 2 = $ _____

   c $39 - 25$ think $39 - $ ____ $- 5 = $ ____

   d $28 - 17$ think $28 - $ ____ $- 7 = $ ____

3   **Answer**:

   a $44 - 12 = $ _____

   b $39 - 16 = $ _____

   c $49 - 26 = $ _____

   d $28 - 11 = $ _____

4   Find the **missing numbers**:

   a $20 - $ ____ $= 11$

   b $26 - $ ____ $= 10$

   c $44 - $ ____ $= 22$

   d $39 - $ ____ $= 18$

5   **Complete**: $28 - 5 = $ _____

6   Use the **jump strategy** to complete:

   $38 - 14$ think $38 - $ ____ $- 4 = $ ____

7   **Answer**: $35 - 13 = $ _____

8   Find the **missing number**: $40 - $ ____ $= 28$

9   Draw a **picture** to show the number sentence:

   $43 - 22 = $ ____ and solve it.

Subtraction to 99

1   **Complete**:

   a   4 tens and 3 units – 1 ten and 2 units = _____

   b   7 tens and 8 units – 5 tens and 3 units = _____

   c   9 tens and 6 units – 6 tens and 2 units = _____

   d   5 tens and 5 units – 2 tens and 3 units = _____

2   **Find**:

   a $79 - 36 = $ _____

   b $57 - 23 = $ _____

   c $65 - 12 = $ _____

   d $86 - 35 = $ _____

3   **Complete**:

   a   45 birds, 23 flew away. How many **left**? _____

   b   98 flowers, 73 picked. How many **left**? _____

   c   56 books, 31 sold. How many **left**? _____

   d   55 chocolates in a box, 43 eaten. How many **left**? _____

4   Find the **missing numbers**:

   a $63 - $ ____ $= 51$

   b $75 - $ ____ $= 44$

   c $98 - $ ____ $= 76$

   d $88 - $ ____ $= 33$

5   **Complete**: 8 tens and 5 units – 6 tens and 2 units = _____

6   **Find**: $75 - 33 = $ ____

7   **Complete**: 58 apples, 26 eaten. How many **left**? ____

8   Find the **missing number**: $89 - $ ____ $= 55$

9   Cooper had 47 lollipops. He gave 5 away and had 43 left.

   What is **wrong** with Cooper's story? _____

   How many did he really have **left**? _____

Subtraction to 99 vertically

1 Solve:

  a $38 - 23 =$ _____   b $45 - 24 =$ _____

  c $56 - 12 =$ _____   d $88 - 71 =$ _____

2 Complete:

  a   9 t + 3 u   b   8 t + 4 u
      − 7 t + 1 u   − 3 t + 2 u

  c   8 t + 8 u   d   6 t + 3 u
      − 4 t + 4 u   − 4 t + 1 u

3 Complete:

a
T	U
6	9
− 1	4

b
T	U
8	7
− 4	6

c
T	U
3	9
+ 2	6

d
T	U
8	5
+ 6	3

4 Find the **missing digits**:

a
```
    7  3
 − [ ] 2
 ─────────
    4 [ ]
```

b
```
    8  6
 − 2 [ ]
 ─────────
 [ ] 1
```

c
```
 [ ][ ]
 −  3  3
 ─────────
    5  5
```

d
```
    9 [ ]
 −  2  7
 ─────────
 [ ] 1
```

5 Solve: $67 - 25 =$ _____

6 Complete: 8 t + 7 u
              − 5 t + 2 u

7 Complete:
T	U
4	7
− 3	5

8 Find the **missing digits**:
```
    8 [ ]
 −  2  3
 ─────────
 [ ] 3
```

9 Start at 98, subtract 42 then subtract 33.

   What is the **final answer**? _____

Subtracting 2-digit numbers

1 Find:

  a $79 - 36 =$ _____

  b $75 - 31 =$ _____

  c $64 - 43 =$ _____

  d $38 - 33 =$ _____

2 Use the **jump strategy** to find:

  a $39 - 25 = 39 - 20 -$ ____ $=$ ____

  b $46 - 33 = 46 -$ ____ $- 3 =$ ____

  c $75 - 44 = 75 -$ ____ $- 4 =$ ____

  d $86 - 26 = 86 - 20 -$ ____ $=$ ____

3 Find the **difference between**:

  a 59 and 27 _____

  b 83 and 51 _____

  c 98 and 27 _____

  d 88 and 46 _____

4 Complete:

  a $70 - 15 =$ _____

  b $80 - 27 =$ _____

  c $90 - 46 =$ _____

  d $50 - 38 =$ _____

5 Find: $88 - 27 =$ _____

6 Use the **jump strategy** to find:

  $88 - 47 = 88 -$ ____ $- 7 =$ ____

7 Find the **difference between**:

  78 and 27 _____

8 Complete:

  $60 - 56 =$ _____

9 Find the **missing digits**:

a
```
 [ ][ ]
 −  2  6
 ─────────
    1  2
```

b
```
    5  0
 − [ ][ ]
 ─────────
    2  5
```

Links between addition & subtraction

1 Complete:

a 14 + 5 = 19   19 – ___ = 5   19 – ___ = 14
b 5 + 11 = 16   16 – ___ = 5   16 – ___ = 11
c 12 + 8 = 20   20 – ___ = 8   20 – ___ = 12
d 7 + 6 = 13   13 – ___ = 6   13 – ___ = 7

2 Complete:

a 27 – 16 = _____   16 + _____ = 27
b 49 – 23 = _____   23 + _____ = 49
c 86 – 41 = _____   41 + _____ = 86
d 78 – 35 = _____   35 + _____ = 78

3 Complete each question and **check** the **answers**:

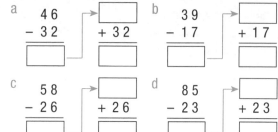

4 Complete each question and **check** the **answers**:

a   5 9   b   7 4
     – 2 6   +   – 5 1   +
   _____ _____   _____ _____

c   8 6   d   6 8
     – 4 3   +   – 5 3   +
   _____ _____   _____ _____

5 Complete:

13 + 6 = 19   19 – ___ = 6   19 – ___ = 13

6 Complete: 56 – 23 = ____   23 + ____ = 56

7 Complete and **check** the **answer**:   7 4

                                             – 3 2   + 3 2

8 Complete and **check** the **answer**:   8 8
                                             – 3 3   + ____

9 Is 98 – 36 the same as 53? _____

Show how you checked: _____

_____

_____

Multiplication as repeated addition

1 Complete:

a 7 + 7 + 7 + 7 +7 = _____
b 3 + 3 + 3 + 3 + 3 + 3 + 3 + 3 = _____
c 5 + 5 + 5 = _____
d 10 + 10 + 10 + 10 + 10 + 10 = _____

2 Complete:

a 4 + 4 + 4 = _____
   3 × 4 = _____
b 8 + 8 + 8 + 8 + 8 = _____
   5 × 8 = _____
c 9 + 9 + 9 + 9 = _____
   4 × 9 = _____
d 2 + 2 + 2 + 2 + 2 + 2 + 2 + 2 = _____
   8 × 2 = _____

3 **Expand** and complete:

a 2 × 7 = ___ + ___ = _____
b 5 × 6 = ___ + ___ + ___ + ___ + ___ = _____
c 4 × 10 = ___ + ___ + ___ + ___ = _____
d 3 × 9 = ___ + ___ + ___ = _____

4 **True or false**?

a 6 × 3 = 3 + 3 + 3   _____
b 4 × 8 = 8 + 8 + 8 + 8   _____
c 3 × 10 = 10 + 10 + 10   _____
d 7 × 2 = 2 + 2 + 2   _____

5 Complete:

9 + 9 + 9 + 9 = _____

6 Complete: 7 + 7 + 7 + 7 = 4 × 7 = _____

7 **Expand** and complete:

5 × 4 = ___ + ___ + ___ + ___ + ___ = _____

8 **True or false**?

4 × 6 = 4 + 4 + 4 + 4   _____

9 Write all the different **number sentences** to make 12, using **repeated addition**.

_____

_____

_____

Multiplication as groups

1 Count to find the **total number** of counters:

a OO OO OO   b OO OO
  OO OO OO   O O
  OO OO OO

_____   _____

c OOO OOO OOO   d OOO OOO
   OO   OO   OO   OOO OOO
                 OOO OOO

_____   _____

2 Complete the **number sentence** for:

a OO OO OO OO
  OO OO OO OO   4 groups of ___ = ___

b OO OO OO OO
  O   O   O   O   ___ groups of ___ = ___

c OOO OOO OOO
   OO   OO   OO
    OOO OOO
     OO   OO   ___ groups of ___ = ___

d   O   O   O
   O   O   O
   O   O   O
   O   O   O
   O   O   O   ___ groups of ___ = ___

3 Write the **number sentence** and solve:

a 4 groups of 2 fish = _____
b 3 groups of 6 cats = _____
c 5 groups of 10 pencils = _____
d 2 groups of 5 cards = _____

4 **Solve**:

a 5 groups of 3 = _____
b 7 groups of 1 = _____
c 6 groups of 10 = _____
d 8 groups of 2 = _____

5 Count the **total number** of counters:

OO OO OO OO OO OO OO _____

6 Complete the **number sentence** and solve:

OO OO OO OO
OO OO OO OO   ___ groups of ___ = ___

7 Write the **number sentence** and solve:

6 groups of 2 chickens = _____

8 **Solve**: 10 groups of 3 = _____

9 Draw a **picture** to show 12 **groups of** 3 children:

How many children altogether? _____

Multiplication as arrays

1 Complete a **number sentence** for:

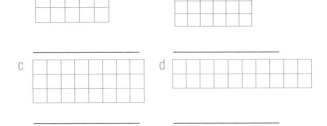

3 rows of 3 = ___   4 rows of 6 = ___

2 rows of 5 = ___   3 rows of 7 = ___

2 Write a **number sentence** for each of the following:

a   b

_____   _____

c   d

_____   _____

3 **Complete**:

a 3 **rows** of 8 = _____
b 6 **rows** of 2 = _____
c 9 **rows** of 1 = _____
d 10 **rows** of 4 = _____

4 **Shade** the **boxes** to show:

a 2 × 3 =   b 4 × 3 =

c 1 × 6 =   d 3 × 5 =

5 Complete the **number sentence** for:

4 rows of 8 = _____

6 Write a **number sentence** for:

_____

7 **Complete**: 2 **rows** of 7 = _____

8 **Shade** the **boxes** to show 3 × 3 = _____

9 **Shade** the **grids** to show 3 different ways to make 6, e.g. 1 × 6

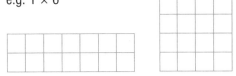

Multiplication facts × 2

1 Complete the **number sentences** using the pictures:

a [X X X / X X X]　　b [X X X X / X X X X] [X X X / X X X]

3 groups of 2 = _____　　7 groups of 2 = _____

c [X X X X X X X X X X / X X X X X X X X X X]

10 groups of ___ = ___

d [X X / X X]

2 groups of ___ = ___

2 Use the array to complete the **number sentences**:

○○○○○○○○○○
○○○○○○○○○○

a 10 × 2 = _____　　b 6 × 2 = _____
c 5 × 2 = _____　　d 7 × 2 = _____

3 Look at the arrays and write a **number sentence**:

a [grid]　　b [grid]

_____　　_____

c [grid]　　d [grid]

_____　　_____

4 Draw an **array** to show:

a 3 × 2 =　　b 10 × 2 =

c 4 × 2 =　　d 1 × 2 =

5 Complete the **number sentence** using the picture:

6 groups of ___ = ___　[X X X X X X / X X X X X X]

6 Use the **array** to complete the **number sentence**:

8 × 2 = _____　○○○○○○○○○○ / ○○○○○○○○○○

7 Look at the array and write a **number sentence**:

[grid] _____

8 Draw an **array** for 2 × 2 = _____

9 Complete the **grid**:

×	2	4	7	10
2				

Multiplication facts × 3

1 Find how many **corners** there are on:

△△△△△△△△△△

a 1 triangle: _____　　b 2 triangles: _____
c 5 triangles: _____　　d 10 triangles: _____

2 Write a **number sentence** to describe the arrays:

a ○○○ / ○○○ / ○○○　　b ○○○○○ / ○○○○○ / ○○○○○

_____　　_____

c ○○○ / ○○○ / ○○○ / ○○○ / ○○○ / ○○○ / ○○○　　d ○○○ / ○○○

_____

3 Complete:

a 3 **groups of** 2 = 2 groups of 2 + 2 = _____
b 3 **groups of** 5 = 2 groups of 5 + 5 = _____
c 3 **groups of** 10 = 2 groups of 10 + 10 = _____
d 3 **groups of** 7 = 2 groups of 7 + 7 = _____

4 Complete:

a 1 × 3 = _____　　b 3 × 3 = _____
c 3 × 10 = _____　　d 3 × 7 = _____

5 Find how many **corners** there are on 6 triangles.

_____　△△△△△

6 Write a **number sentence** to describe:

○○○ / ○○○ / ○○○ / ○○○　_____

7 Complete:

3 groups of 9 = 2 groups of 9 + 9 = _____

8 Complete: 3 × 5 = _____

9 Complete the wheel:

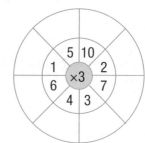

Multiplication facts × 4

1 Complete the **number sentences** by using the diagrams:

a ▯▯▯▯▯   b ▯▯▯▯▯▯▯▯

5 groups of ___ = ___   8 groups of ___ = ___

c ▯▯   d ▯▯▯▯▯▯

___ groups of ___ = ___   ___ groups of ___ = ___

2 Use the **array** to complete:

○○○○○○○○○○
○○○○○○○○○○
○○○○○○○○○○
○○○○○○○○○○

a 3 × 4 = ____   b 7 × 4 = ____
c 10 × 4 = ____   d 4 × 4 = ____

3 Complete the **pairs**:

a 2 × 4 = ____ = 4 × 2 b 7 × 4 = ____ = 4 × 7
c 9 × 4 = ____ = 4 × 9 d 1 × 4 = ____ = 4 × 1

4 **Complete**:

a 3 × 4 = _____   b _____ × 4 = 40
c _____ × 4 = 20   d 8 × 4 = _____

5 Complete the **number sentence** using the diagram:

▯▯▯▯▯▯▯   ___ groups of ___ = ___

6 Use the **diagram** to complete: 5 × 4 = ____

7 Complete the **pair**: 10 × 4 = ____ = 4 × 10

8 **Complete**: ____ × 4 = 4

9 a Shade the **tables** of 2. b Circle the **tables** of 4.
c What did you **discover**?

_____

_____

_____

1	2	3	4	5	6	7	8	9	10
11	12	13	14	15	16	17	18	19	20
21	22	23	24	25	26	27	28	29	30
31	32	33	34	35	36	37	38	39	40
41	42	43	44	45	46	47	48	49	50
51	52	53	54	55	56	57	58	59	60
61	62	63	64	65	66	67	68	69	70
71	72	73	74	75	76	77	78	79	80
81	82	83	84	85	86	87	88	89	90
91	92	93	94	95	96	97	98	99	100

Multiplication facts × 5

1 Use diagrams to complete the **number sentences**:

1 group of 5 = ____   7 groups of 5 = ____

3 group of 5 = ____   5 groups of 5 = ____

2 Use the **array** to complete:

a 9 × 5 = ____
b 4 × 5 = ____
c 8 × 5 = ____
d 2 × 5 = ____

3 Draw a **diagram** to show:

a 1 × 5 = ____   b 6 × 5 = ____

c 2 × 5 = ____   d 3 × 5 = ____

4 Complete the **tables**:

a

×	1	2	3	4
5				

b

×	5	6	7	8
5				

c

×	7	8	9	10
5				

d

×	1	3	5	7
5				

5 Use the diagram to complete the **number sentence**:

6 groups of 5 = ____

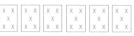

6 Use the diagram to **complete**:

5 × 5 = ____

7 Draw a **diagram** to show: 4 × 5 = ____

8 **Complete**:

×	2	4	6	8
5				

9 It cost 1 person $5 to enter the park.
What is the **total cost** if 5 people entered the park?

_____

Units

Multiplication facts × 6

1 If 1 insect has 6 legs, what is the **total number** of legs on:

a 5 insects? ____

b 8 insects? ____

c 10 insects? ____

d 3 insects? ____

2 **Complete**:

a $1 \times 6 = \square = 6 \times 1$

b $10 \times 6 = \square = 6 \times \square$

c $8 \times 6 = \square = 6 \times \square$

d $2 \times 6 = \square = \square \times 2$

3 Use the **array** to answer the equations:

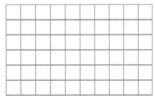

a $4 \times 6 =$ ____　　b $6 \times 6 =$ ____

c $9 \times 6 =$ ____　　d $7 \times 6 =$ ____

4 **Complete**:

a $\begin{array}{r} 6 \\ \times\ 2 \\ \hline \end{array}$　　b $\begin{array}{r} 7 \\ \times\ 6 \\ \hline \end{array}$

c $\begin{array}{r} 4 \\ \times\ 6 \\ \hline \end{array}$　　d $\begin{array}{r} 6 \\ \times\ 9 \\ \hline \end{array}$

5 If 1 insect has 6 legs, what is the **total number** of legs on 4 insects?

6 **Complete**:

$7 \times 6 = \square = 6 \times \square$

7 Use an **array** to answer: $5 \times 6 =$ ____

8 $\begin{array}{r} 1\ 0 \\ \times\ \ 6 \\ \hline \end{array}$

9 **Complete**:

Multiplication facts × 7

1 1 week has 7 days. Use the calendar to help find the **number of days** in:

a 5 weeks: ____

b 7 weeks: ____

c 3 weeks: ____

d 10 weeks: ____

June						
S	M	T	W	Th	F	S
						1
2	3	4	5	6	7	8
9	10	11	12	13	14	15
16	17	18	19	20	21	22
23	24	25	26	27	28	2
30						

July						
S	M	T	W	Th	F	S
	1	2	3	4	5	6
7	8	9	10	11	12	13
14	15	16	17	18	19	20
21	22	23	24	25	26	27
28	29	30	31			

August						
S	M	T	W	Th	F	S
					1	2	3
4	5	6	7	8	9	10
11	12	13	14	15	16	17
18	19	20	21	22	23	24
25	26	27	28	29	30	31

2 **Complete**:

a $7 \times 7 =$ ____　　b $5 \times 7 =$ ____

c $3 \times 7 =$ ____　　d $1 \times 7 =$ ____

3 **Complete**:

a 2 **groups of** 7 = ____

b 4 **groups of** 7 = ____

c 9 **groups of** 7 = ____

d 6 **groups of** 7 = ____

4 **Complete**:

a $\begin{array}{r} 1\ 0 \\ \times\ \ 7 \\ \hline \end{array}$　　b $\begin{array}{r} 9 \\ \times\ 7 \\ \hline \end{array}$

c $\begin{array}{r} 2 \\ \times\ 7 \\ \hline \end{array}$　　d $\begin{array}{r} 7 \\ \times\ 7 \\ \hline \end{array}$

5 1 week has 7 days. How **many days** in 6 weeks? ____

6 **Complete**: $8 \times 7 =$ ____

7 3 **groups of** 7 = ____

8 **Complete**: $\begin{array}{r} 4 \\ \times\ 7 \\ \hline \end{array}$

9 **Complete** the wheel:

Multiplication facts × 8

1   1 spider has 8 legs. **How many legs** have:

a   10 spiders? ____

b   6 spiders? ____

c   4 spiders? ____

d   3 spiders? ____

2   **Complete**:

a $5 \times 8 =$ ____

b $7 \times 8 =$ ____

c $8 \times 8 =$ ____

d $9 \times 8 =$ ____

3   Find the **missing digits**:

a $1 \times 8 = \square$

b $6 \times \square = 48$

c $3 \times \square = 24$

d $\square \times 7 = 56$

4   **Complete**:

a   The **product of** 2 and 8 = _____

b   The **product of** 9 and 8 = _____

c   The **product of** 6 and 8 = _____

d   The **product of** 5 and 8 = _____

5   How many **legs** are there on 7 spiders? _____

6   **Complete**:

$3 \times 8 =$ ____

7   Find the **missing digit**:

$8 \times \square = 64$

8   The **product** of 4 and 8 is _____.

9   Use an **open number line** to find 3×8.

Multiplication facts × 9

1   Use the **array** to help answer the following:

a   8 **groups** of 9 = ____

b   4 **groups** of 9 = ____

c   9 **groups** of 9 = ____

d   3 **groups** of 9 = ____

2   **Complete**:

a $7 \times 9 =$ ____   b $6 \times 9 =$ ____

c $1 \times 9 =$ ____   d $10 \times 9 =$ ____

3   Find the **missing digits**:

a $1 \times 9 = 10 - \square = \square$

b $2 \times 9 = 20 - \square = \square$

c $3 \times 9 = 30 - \square = \square$

d $4 \times 9 = 40 - \square = \square$

4   Write the **number sentence** for each of the answers from the 9 times table:

a   63 = _____

b   81 = _____

c   27 = _____

d   54 = _____

5   5 **groups** of 9 = _____

6   **Complete**: $4 \times 9 =$ _____

7   **Complete**: $5 \times 9 = 50 - \square = \square$

8   Write the **number sentence** for the answer from the 9 times table:

45 = _____

9   Look at these answers to the 9 times table:

9, 18, 27, 36

What do you find if you **add the digits** together for each of the answers?

i.e. 18 is $1 + 8 =$ ____

_____

_____

Multiplication facts × 10

1 A Base 10 flat is a 10 × 10 grid. Use this to help **complete** the following answers:

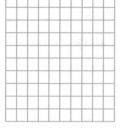

a 5 × 10 = _____

b 7 × 10 = _____

c 8 × 10 = _____

d 10 × 10 = _____

2 Find the **missing digits**:

a 6 × ☐ = 60   b ☐ × 10 = 10

c ☐ × 10 = 40   d 9 × 10 = ☐

3 Find the **product of**:

a 7 and 10 = ____

b 2 and 10 = ____

c 5 and 10 = ____

d 8 and 10 = ____

4 Complete the **tables**:

a

×	1	2	3	4
10				

b

×	5	6	7	8
10				

c

×	7	8	9	10
10				

d

×	9	7	5	3
10				

5 **Complete**: 4 × 10 = _____

6 **Complete**: ☐ × 10 = 70

7 Find the **product** of 6 and 10. _____

8 Complete the **table**:

×	8	6	4	2
10				

9 If there are 10 pencils in 1 packet, how many pencils are in **7 packets**?

_____

Mixed multiplication facts

1 **Complete**:

a 4 × 6 = _____   b 8 × 7 = _____

c 3 × 5 = _____   d 1 × 9 = _____

2 **Complete**:

a   6   b   1 0
  × 3   × 2
  _____   _____

c   5   d   8
  × 6   × 8
  _____   _____

3 **Complete**:

a 5 × 4 = ☐ = 2 × ☐

b 3 × 6 = ☐ = 2 × ☐

c 4 × 10 = ☐ = 5 × 8

d 3 × ☐ = ☐ = 1 × 9

4 Draw **arrays** to show:

a 1 × 7 = ____   b 3 × 7 = ____

c 2 × 9 = ____   d 8 × 4 = ____

5 **Complete**: 10 × 10 = _____

6 **Complete**:   7
      × 5
     _____

7 Find the **missing numbers**:

3 × ☐ = ☐ = 6 × 2

8 Draw an **array** to show: 4 × 5 = ____

9 **Complete the table**:

×	2	4	5	6
3				
6				
9				

Excel Start Up Maths Year 2

☞ Answers on page 87

Division as sharing

1 Use the pictures to **share**:

a 9 by 3

b 6 by 2

c 12 by 4

d 10 by 5

2 **Complete** the following:

a share between 2

= ____

b share between 3

= ____

c share between 5

= ____

d share between 1

= ____

3 **Complete**:

a 21 **shared between** 3 = ____

b 18 **shared between** 6 = ____

c 20 **shared between** 10 = ____

d 25 **shared between** 5 = ____

4 **Complete**:

a 4 girls **share** 20 apples. One share = _____

b 6 teachers **share** 30 biscuits. One share = _____

c 10 children **share** 50 stickers. One share = ____

d 4 boys **share** 8 tennis balls. One share = _____

5 8 **shared** between 4:

= _____

6 **Share** between 4:

= _____

7 Complete: 27 **shared between** 9 = _____

8 5 children **share** 10 cupcakes. One share = _____

9 Draw a **picture** of 20 apples shared by 4 children.

Division as repeated subtraction

1 How many **groups of 2** can be taken from each of the following:

a

b

_____   _____

c

d

_____   _____

2 There are 16 apples in the basket. How many **times** can I take:

a 2 apples?   ____ times

b 4 apples?   ____ times

c 8 apples?   ____ times

d 16 apples?   ____ times

3 How many **times** can I take:

a 10 pens from 90 pens? ____

b 4 balls from 40 balls? ____

c 6 books from 36 books? ____

d 8 rulers from 16 rulers? ____

4 **How many**:

a 5s in 25? ____

b 8s in 48? ____

c 10s in 100? ____

d 3s in 18? ____

5 How many **groups** of 2 can be made from:

_____

6 There are 15 apples in the basket. How many **times** can I take 3 apples? ____ times

7 How many **times** can I take 3 pencils from 30 pencils?

____ times

8 **How many** 4s in 24? ____

9 Show using **subtraction** how 5 children would **share** 35 pencils.

35 – _____

Division by 2

1 Use the **number line** to find the answers:

```
0  2  4  6  8  10 12 14 16 18 20
```

a How many 2s are in 4? ____
b How many 2s are in 8? ____
c How many 2s are in 16? ____
d How many 2s are in 20? ____

2 Use the **arrays** to find:

a $12 ÷ 2 =$ ____   b $6 ÷ 2 =$ ____

c $8 ÷ 2 =$ ____   d $10 ÷ 2 =$ ____

3 Draw **arrays** to show:
a $4 ÷ 2 = 2$ b $2 ÷ 2 = 1$

c $14 ÷ 2 = 7$ d $16 ÷ 2 = 8$

4 **Find**:
a 6 **divided** by 2 = ____
b 8 **divided** by 2 = ____
c 20 **divided** by 2 = ____
d 18 **divided** by 2 = ____

5 Using the **number line**, how many 2s are in 18? ____

```
0  2  4  6  8  10 12 14 16 18 20
```

6 Using the **array**: $4 ÷ 2 =$ _____

7 Draw **an array** to show: $18 ÷ 2 = 9$

8 Find: 18 **divided** by 2 = ____

9 Write 3 **different division equations** that include the number 12.

_____ _____ _____

Division by 3

1 How many **times** can I take 3 apples from:
a 9 apples?   ____ times
b 12 apples?   ____ times
c 15 apples?   ____ times
d 3 apples?   ____ times

2 **Complete**:
a $30 ÷ 3 =$ ____
b $18 ÷ 3 =$ ____
c $21 ÷ 3 =$ ____
d $6 ÷ 3 =$ ____

3 **Complete**:
a $3 × 1 = 3$ $3 ÷ 1 =$ ____
b $3 × 8 = 24$ $24 ÷ 3 =$ ____
c $3 × 9 = 27$ $27 ÷ 3 =$ ____
d $3 × 5 = 15$ $15 ÷ 3 =$ ____

4 Draw a **picture** to show:
a $9 ÷ 3 =$ ____   b $6 ÷ 3 =$ ____

c $12 ÷ 3 =$ ____   d $21 ÷ 3 =$ ____

5 How many **times** can I take 3 apples from 6 apples?

_____ times

6 **Complete**: $3 ÷ 3 =$ _____

7 **Complete**: $3 × 3 = 9$ $9 ÷ 3 =$ _____

8 Draw a **picture** to show: $3 ÷ 3 =$ _____

9 Write a **word problem** for the number sentence:

$30 ÷ 3 = 10$

_____

_____

_____

UNIT 51

See START UPS page 4

Division: links with multiplication facts

1 Use the first number sentence to complete the **other two**:

a $6 \times 4 = 24$ $24 \div 4 = $ _____ $24 \div 6 = $ _____

b $5 \times 8 = 40$ $40 \div 5 = $ _____ $40 \div 8 = $ _____

c $9 \times 6 = 54$ $54 \div 9 = $ _____ $54 \div 6 = $ _____

d $10 \times 3 = 30$ $30 \div 10 = $ _____ $30 \div 3 = $ _____

2 Use the first number sentence to complete the **other two**:

a $70 \div 7 = 10$ ___ $\times 7 = 70$ ___ $\times 10 = 70$

b $18 \div 3 = 6$ ___ $\times 3 = 18$ ___ $\times 6 = 18$

c $32 \div 8 = 4$ ___ $\times 4 = 32$ ___ $\times 8 = 32$

d $30 \div 6 = 5$ ___ $\times 5 = 30$ ___ $\times 6 = 30$

3 Find how many **groups of**:

a 3 fish can be made from 21 fish   _____

b 9 hats can be made from 45 hats   _____

c 10 books can be made from 50 books _____

d 6 toys can be made from 24 toys   _____

4 Write **1 multiplication** and **1 division** fact to describe each of the arrays:

a ○○○○○○○   b ○○○○○
                   ○○○○○

_____   _____

_____   _____

c ○○○○   d ○○○○
  ○○○○   ○○○○
  ○○○○   ○○○○
                   ○○○○
                   ○○○○

_____   _____

_____   _____

5 Use the first number sentence to complete the **other two**:

$6 \times 7 = 42$ $42 \div 6 = $ _____ $42 \div 7 = $ _____

6 Use the first number sentence to complete the **other two**:

$90 \div 9 = 10$ _____ $\times 10 = 90$ _____ $\times 9 = 90$

7 Find how many **groups of** 5 balls can be made from 55 balls. _____

8 Write **1 multiplication** and **1 division** fact to describe:

○○○○○○○○○○○○
○○○○○○○○○○○○

_____   _____

9 Write a **word question** to match the number sentence: $3 \times 4 = 12$

_____

_____

UNIT 52

See START UPS page 4

Division with remainders

1 Make the following **groups**:

a of 2 stars   b of 3 circles

☆☆☆☆   ○○○
☆☆☆   ○○○○
                       ○○○

_____ groups   _____ groups
_____ stars left over   _____ circles left over

c of 4 squares   d of 6 hearts

▢▢▢▢   ♡♡♡♡
▢▢▢▢   ♡♡♡♡
▢▢

_____ groups   _____ groups
_____ squares left over _____ hearts left over

2 Answer the questions using the diagram:

a How many **groups of** 4? _____

b How many **groups of** 5? _____

c How many **groups of** 3? _____ remainder _____

d How many **groups of** 6? _____ remainder _____

3 How many **groups of**:

a 5 fish in 13 fish? _____ r _____

b 9 frogs in 30 frogs? _____ r _____

c 6 turtles in 25 turtles? _____ r _____

d 3 lizards in 20 lizards? _____ r _____

4 **Complete**:

a $10 \div 3 = $ _____   b $11 \div 4 = $ _____

c $22 \div 8 = $ _____   d $8 \div 5 = $ _____

5 Make **groups of** 4 squares:

▢▢▢▢▢   _____ groups
▢▢▢▢▢   _____ squares left over
▢▢▢▢▢

6 How many **groups of** 7?

○○○○
○○○○
○○○○   _____ remainder _____
○○○○
○○○○

7 How many **groups of** 4 snakes in 25 snakes?

_____

8 **Complete**: $15 \div 4 = $ _____

9 There is a pile of 33 magazines. How many **sets of** 4 magazines are there?

_____

Rounding numbers (1)

1 Round each number to the **nearest ten**:

   a   49 _____

   b   61 _____

   c   73 _____

   d   98 _____

2 Round each number to the **nearest hundred**:

   a   190 _____

   b   212 _____

   c   385 _____

   d   405 _____

3 **Answer** the following:

   a   Is 612 closer to 600 or 700? _____

   b   Is 111 closer to 100 or 200? _____

   c   Is 375 closer to 300 or 400? _____

   d   Is 893 closer to 800 or 900? _____

4 **True or false?**

   a   779 rounded to the **nearest hundred** is 800. _____

   b   638 rounded to the **nearest ten** is 640. _____

   c   852 rounded to the **nearest hundred** is 850. _____

   d   925 rounded to the **nearest ten** is 1000. _____

5 Round 17 to the **nearest ten**. _____

6 Round 777 to the **nearest hundred**. _____

7 Is 463 **closer** to 400 or 500? _____

8 **True or false?**

   415 rounded to the **nearest hundred** is 400. _____

9 Is 1475 **closer** to 1400 or 1500? **Explain.**

_____

_____

_____

Rounding numbers (2)

1 Round each number to the **nearest ten**:

   a   491 _____

   b   314 _____

   c   606 _____

   d   121 _____

2 Round each number to the **nearest hundred**:

   a   296 _____

   b   301 _____

   c   475 _____

   d   862 _____

3 Round each of the numbers to the **nearest hundred**:

   a   3572 _____

   b   4669 _____

   c   5201 _____

   d   9516 _____

4 Round each of the numbers to the **nearest ten** and use these to estimate the answer:

   a   31 + 69 = ____ + ____ = _____

   b   11 + 72 = ____ + ____ = _____

   c   39 + 47 = ____ + ____ = _____

   d   79 + 12 = ____ + ____ = _____

5 Round 896 to the **nearest ten**. _____

6 Round 728 to the **nearest hundred**. _____

7 Round 1193 to the **nearest hundred**. _____

8 Round each number to the **nearest ten** and then use these to estimate the answer:

   71 + 58 = _____ + _____ = _____

9 Estimate the **total number** of seeds by rounding the numbers to the **nearest ten** and then adding:

19 Seeds   11 Seeds   23 Seeds   17 Seeds

_____

Using number lines

1 Use the **jump strategy** with the number line to solve the addition equations.

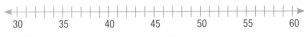

a   31 + 20 = _____   b   42 + 13 = _____
c   33 + 21 = _____   d   39 + 12 = _____

2 Use the **jump strategy** with the number line to solve the subtraction equations.

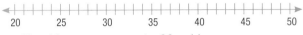

a   49 − 12 = _____   b   38 − 11 = _____
c   47 − 21 = _____   d   48 − 23 = _____

3 Use the **number line** to find:

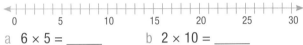

a   6 × 5 = _____   b   2 × 10 = _____
c   4 × 5 = _____   d   5 × 5 = _____

4 Use the **number line** to find:

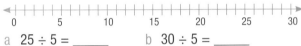

a   25 ÷ 5 = _____   b   30 ÷ 5 = _____
c   15 ÷ 5 = _____   d   20 ÷ 5 = _____

5 Use the **jump strategy** with the number line to solve:
68 + 13 = _____

6 Use the **jump strategy** with the number line to solve:
52 − 21 = _____

7 Use the **number line** to find: 7 × 5 = _____

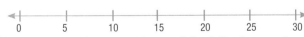

8 Use the **number line** to find: 25 ÷ 5 = _____

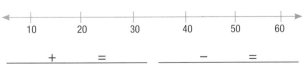

9 Write **4 equations** based around the following number line:

_____ + _____ = _____   _____ − _____ = _____

_____ × _____ = _____   _____ ÷ _____ = _____

Inverse operations

1 Check the addition facts by using **subtraction**:

a   24 + 8 = 32   32 − _____ = _____
b   53 + 9 = 62   62 − _____ = _____
c   37 + 8 = 45   45 − _____ = _____
d   17 + 6 = 23   23 − _____ = _____

2 Check the subtraction facts by using **addition**:

a   19 − 7 = 12   12 + _____ = _____
b   25 − 14 = 11   11 + _____ = _____
c   37 − 28 = 9   9 + _____ = _____
d   42 − 23 = 19   19 + _____ = _____

3 Write a **division fact** from each multiplication fact:

a   9 × 5 = 45   45 ÷ _____ = _____
b   10 × 6 = 60   60 ÷ _____ = _____
c   3 × 8 = 24   24 ÷ _____ = _____
d   4 × 7 = 28   28 ÷ _____ = _____

4 Write a **multiplication fact** from the division fact:

a   16 ÷ 8 = 2   2 × _____ = _____
b   24 ÷ 4 = 6   6 × _____ = _____
c   40 ÷ 8 = 5   5 × _____ = _____
d   56 ÷ 7 = 8   8 × _____ = _____

5 Check the addition fact by using **subtraction**:

17 + 19 = 36   36 − _____ = _____

6 Check the subtraction fact by using **addition**:

47 − 12 = 35   35 + _____ = _____

7 Write a **division fact** from:

5 × 4 = 20   20 ÷ _____ = _____

8 Write a **multiplication fact** from:

36 ÷ 6 = 6   6 × _____ = _____

9 Cross off **all of the answers** in the grid to see which row is the winner. _____

a   5 × 2
b   12 ÷ 6
c   7 + 6
d   9 − 5
e   2 × 8
f   20 ÷ 4
g   7 + 2

A	16	6	2
B	4	10	7
C	9	5	13

Missing numbers

1. Write the **missing numbers** in the spaces:

   a $8 + \square = 17$

   b $9 + \square = 15$

   c $11 + \square = 22$

   d $21 + \square = 40$

2. Write the **missing numbers** in the spaces:

   a $12 - \square = 8$

   b $11 - \square = 6$

   c $19 - \square = 10$

   d $21 - \square = 14$

3. Write the **missing numbers** in the spaces:

   a $4 \times \square = 24$

   b $7 \times \square = 49$

   c $5 \times \square = 35$

   d $8 \times \square = 32$

4. Write the **missing numbers** in the spaces:

   a $50 \div \square = 10$

   b $18 \div \square = 9$

   c $16 \div \square = 4$

   d $100 \div \square = 10$

5. Write the **missing number** in the space:

   $15 + \square = 32$

6. Write the **missing number** in the space:

   $25 - \square = 10$

7. Write the **missing number** in the space:

   $3 \times \square = 27$

8. Write the **missing number** in the space:

   $12 \div \square = 3$

9. Use +, −, × or ÷ to make the **number sentences** correct:

   a $4 \;\square\; 5 = 20$

   b $9 \;\square\; 11 = 20$

   c $30 \;\square\; 7 = 23$

   d $8 \;\square\; 3 = 24$

Calculators addition and subtraction

1. Use a **calculator** to find the answer to:

   a $28 + 56 = $ _____

   b $29 + 55 = $ _____

   c $56 + 95 = $ _____

   d $49 + 68 = $ _____

2. Use a **calculator** to find the answer to:

   a $57 - 38 = $ _____

   b $51 - 49 = $ _____

   c $97 - 65 = $ _____

   d $42 - 29 = $ _____

3. Use a **calculator** to find the answer to:

   a **add** 72 and 56 _____

   b find the **difference** between 86 and 17 _____

   c **subtract** 85 from 93 _____

   d 86 **plus** 38 equals _____

4. Write a **number sentence** and use a **calculator** to find the answers to:

   a Kasey had 60 sweets, she gave 21 away. How many were **left**? _____

   b Mitchel collected 97 cards and 56 coins. How many items did he collect **altogether**? _____

   c Amity counted 79 pieces of Lego in one tub and 56 pieces in another. How many pieces of Lego **altogether**? _____

   d Damon had 96 stickers in a book. He gave 76 away. How many stickers did he have **left**? _____

5. Use a **calculator** to find: $85 + 55 = $ _____

6. Use a **calculator** to find: $98 - 15 = $ _____

7. Use a **calculator** to find the answer:

   90 minus 76 is _____

8. Write a **number sentence** and use a **calculator** to solve:

   Cooper counted 61 nails and 50 screws, how many items did he count **altogether**? _____

9. Find the **missing number**: $51 - \square = 16$

Calculators multiplication and division

1 Use a **calculator** to find the answers to:

  a 17 × 7 = _____

  b 15 × 9 = _____

  c 18 × 3 = _____

  d 12 × 8 = _____

2 Use a **calculator** to find the answers to:

  a 175 ÷ 7 = _____

  b 144 ÷ 4 = _____

  c 354 ÷ 6 = _____

  d 336 ÷ 7 = _____

3 Use a **calculator** to find the answers to:

  a 9 **times** 22 _____

  b 45 **divided** by 3 _____

  c 7 **groups of** 42 _____

  d **how many groups** of 8 in 360 _____

4 Write a **number sentence** and use a **calculator** to find the answer to:

  a Chase has 25 boxes of 6 doughnuts. How many **altogether**? _____

  b India has to share 180 pencils between 5 containers. How many in **each** container? _____

  c Sarah needs to put 135 books into 9 boxes equally. How many in **each** box? _____

  d Tim has 32 bags of 9 small toys. How many small toys **altogether**? _____

5 Use a **calculator** to find: 27 × 8 = _____

6 Use a **calculator** to find: 96 ÷ 6 = _____

7 Use a calculator to find: 8 **groups of** 25 _____

8 Write a **number sentence** and use a **calculator** to find: There are 8 classes of 26 students in Year 1. How many Year 1 students **altogether**? _____

9 Write 3 different **number sentences** using the calculator which have 500 as the answer:

_____

_____

_____

Number sequences 2s and 3s

1 Continue the **number sequences**:

  a 2, 4, 6, ____, ____, ____

  b 10, 12, 14, ____, ____, ____

  c 20, 18, 16, ____, ____, ____

  d 50, 48, 46, ____, ____, ____

2 Continue the **number sequences**:

  a 3, 6, 9, ____, ____, ____

  b 21, 24, 27, ____, ____, ____

  c 30, 27, 24, ____, ____, ____

  d 60, 57, 54, ____, ____, ____

3 Decide if the number sequence is counting by **2s** or **3s**:

  a 4, 6, 8, 10, 12 _____

  b 100, 97, 94, 91, 88 _____

  c 81, 83, 85, 87, 89 _____

  d 62, 65, 71, 74 _____

4 Write a **number sequence** with the following rules:

  a start at 40 and count **forwards** by 2s to 50

  _____

  b start at 50 and count **backwards** by 2s to 40

  _____

  c start at 90 and count **backwards** by 3s to 72

  _____

  d start at 70 and count **forwards** by 3s to 88

  _____

5 **Continue**: 21, 23, 25, 27, ____, ____, ____

6 **Continue**: 10, 13, 16, ____, ____, ____

7 Decide if the number sequence is counting by **2s or 3s**:

  17, 20, 23, 26, 29 _____

8 Start at 3 and count **forwards** by 2s to 11.

  _____

9 Create your own **number sequence** starting at **100**.

  _____

  Write the **rule**: _____

Number sequences 5s and 10s

1 Continue the **number sequences**:

  a   5, 10, 15, ____, ____, ____

  b   50, 55, 60, ____, ____, ____

  c   50, 45, 40, ____, ____, ____

  d   100, 95, 90, ____, ____, ____

2 Continue the **number sequences**:

  a   10, 20, 30, ____, ____, ____

  b   80, 90, 100, ____, ____, ____

  c   100, 90, 80, ____, ____, ____

  d   200, 190, 180, ____, ____, ____

3 Write a **number sequence** with the following rules:

  a   start at 85 and count **forwards** by 5s to 100:

       _____

  b   start at 110 and count **forwards** by 10s to 140:

       _____

  c   start at 100 and count **backwards** by 5s to 80:

       _____

  d   start at 500 and count **backwards** by 10s to 470:

       _____

4 Complete the **number sequences**:

  a   85, ____, ____, 100, 105

  b   90, 80, ____, 60, ____

  c   105, 100, ____, 90, ____

  d   210, ____, 190, ____, 170

5 **Continue**: 150, 155, 160, ____, ____, ____

6 **Continue**: 130, 120, 110, ____, ____, ____

7 Start at 105 and count **forwards** by 5s to 125.

       _____

8 **Complete**: 210, ____, 230, ____, 250

9 Continue the **number sequences**:

  a   82, 87, 92, ____, ____, ____

  b   103, 93, 83, ____, ____, ____

  c   41, 46, 51, ____, ____, ____

Number sequences (1)

1 Continue the **number sequences**:

  a   0, 4, 8, 12, ____, ____, ____

  b   0, 7, 14, 21, ____, ____, ____

  c   0, 9, 18, 27, ____, ____, ____

  d   0, 6, 12, 18, ____, ____, ____

2 Write a **rule** for each of the number sequences:

  a   3, 6, 9, 12, 15 _____

  b   40, 48, 56, 64 _____

  c   30, 36, 42, 48 _____

  d   20, 30, 40, 50 _____

3 For each number sequence, state what the **tenth number** would be:

  a   2, 4, 6, 8, … , ____

  b   3, 6, 9, 12, … , ____

  c   5, 10, 15, 20, … , ____

  d   10, 20, 30, 40, … , ____

4 Complete the following **tables**:

a

+	10	20	30	40
4				

b

+	30	40	50	60
6				

c

+	4	14	24	34
6				

d

+	6	16	26	36
3				

5 **Complete**: 0, 8, 16, 24, ___, ___, ___

6 Write a **rule** for: 50, 55, 60, 65

       _____

7 State what the **tenth term** would be:

     4, 8, 12, 16, … , ____

8 Complete the **table**:

+	14	24	34	44
5				

9 Complete the **number sequence**:

  a   19, ____, 29 ____, 39, 44

  b   What is the **rule**?

       _____

Number sequences (2)

1 Starting at 50, complete the **number sequences**:

a count **forwards** by 5, 5 times: _____

b count **forwards** by 7, 5 times: _____

c count **backwards** by 3, 5 times: _____

d count **backwards** by 4, 5 times: _____

2 Complete the **tables**:

a
+	4	14	24	34
10				

b
+	5	15	25	35
11				

c
+	2	12	22	32
12				

d
+	10	20	30	40
20				

3 For each number sequence, state the **tenth number**:

a 20, 18, 16, 14, … , _____

b 100, 95, 90, 85, … , _____

c 50, 49, 48, 47, … , _____

d 60, 58, 56, 54, … , _____

4 State the **rule** for each number sequence:

a 3, 6, 9, 12 _____

b 40, 42, 44, 46 _____

c 100, 200, 300, 400 _____

d 1, 3, 5, 7 _____

5 Count **forwards** by 3s, 5 times, starting at 50:

50, ____, ____, ____, ____, ____

6 Complete the **table**:

+	3	13	23	33
30				

7 State what the **tenth number** would be for:

100, 98, 96, 94, … , _____

8 Write a **rule** for this pattern: 20, 23, 26, 29

_____

9 Complete the **doubling number pattern** to 64, with a calculator if needed:

2, 4, 8, _____

Number sentences

1 Write a **number sentence** for the pictures and solve:

a ○○○○
○○○○ + ○○○ ○○

_____

b ○○○⊘⊘
○○○⊘

_____

c ○○○ ○○○ ○○○
○○ ○○ ○○

_____

d (○○○)(○○○)(○○○)(○○○)

_____

2 Write a **number sentence** for the word problems and solve:

a the **total** of 35 cats and 22 cats _____

b the **difference** between 46 students and 31 students _____

c the **total** number of balls, if there are 5 buckets with 7 balls in each bucket _____

d 50 grapes **shared** evenly between 5 boys, how many grapes for each boy? _____

3 Find the **missing numbers**:

a 47 − ____ = 32

b ____ + 12 = 25

c 8 × ____ = 40

d 12 ÷ ____ = 3

4 Write a **word problem/story** for each of the number sentences and solve.

a 13 + 12 = _____

b 20 − 9 = _____

c 3 × 7 = _____

d 20 ÷ 4 = _____

5 Write a **number sentence** for the picture and solve:

⊘⊘⊘⊘⊘
⊘○○○○ _____
○○○○○

6 Write a **number sentence** and solve: the total of 15 birds and 11 birds. _____

7 Find the **missing number**: 10 × ____ = 60

8 Write a **word problem/story** and solve:

30 ÷ 5 = _____

9 Write a **number sentence** and solve:

Matthew had: 8 chickens, 2 dogs, 8 fish and 12 birds.

How many pets did he have altogether? _____

_____

Naming fractions (1)

1 **Complete:**

a $\frac{1}{2}$ is ___ **out of** 2 **equal parts**

b $\frac{1}{4}$ is ___ **out of** 4 **equal parts**

c $\frac{3}{4}$ is ___ **out of** 4 **equal parts**

d $\frac{1}{8}$ is ___ **out of** 8 **equal parts**

2 **Complete:**

a $\frac{1}{2}$ is 1 **out of** ___ **equal parts**

b $\frac{3}{8}$ is 3 **out of** ___ **equal parts**

c $\frac{3}{4}$ is 3 **out of** ___ **equal parts**

d $\frac{5}{8}$ is 5 **out of** ___ **equal parts**

3 Complete the **labels** to represent the shaded part of each shape:

a ___ out of ___   b ___ out of ___

c ___ out of ___   d ___ out of ___

4 Complete the **fractions** to represent the shaded part of each shape:

a $\frac{\square}{8}$ b $\frac{\square}{4}$

c $\frac{\square}{2}$ d $\frac{\square}{8}$

5 **Complete:** $\frac{5}{8}$ is ___ **out of** 8 **equal parts**.

6 **Complete:** $\frac{1}{4}$ is 1 **out of** ___ **equal parts**.

7 Complete the **label** to represent the shaded part of the rectangle:

___ out of ___

8 Complete the **fraction** to represent the shaded part of the circle:

$\frac{\square}{2}$

9 Draw a **picture** to show: $\frac{3}{4}$

Naming fractions (2)

1 What **part** of each of the following shapes has been shaded?

 $\frac{\square}{\square}$ b $\frac{\square}{\square}$

c $\frac{\square}{\square}$ d $\frac{\square}{\square}$

2 What **part** of each group has been shaded?

a ●●●○ $\frac{\square}{\square}$ b $\frac{\square}{\square}$

c ▲▲▲▲▲ $\frac{\square}{\square}$ d ★★★★☆ $\frac{\square}{\square}$

3 Shade **part** of each shape to match the given fraction:

a $\frac{1}{2}$ b $\frac{3}{4}$

c $\frac{6}{8}$ d $\frac{2}{2}$

4 Shade **part** of each group to match the given fraction:

a ○○○○ ○○○○ $\frac{1}{8}$ b □□□□ $\frac{4}{4}$

c ☆☆☆☆☆ ☆☆☆☆☆ $\frac{7}{8}$ d △△ $\frac{1}{2}$

5 What **part** of the circle has been shaded?

 $\frac{\square}{\square}$

6 What **part** of the group has been shaded?

 ▲▲▲▲ $\frac{\square}{\square}$

7 Shade **part** of the circle to show:

$\frac{2}{4}$

8 Shade **part** of the group to show:

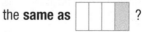 □□□□□□□□ $\frac{6}{8}$

9 Is [ ] the **same as** [ ] ?

Explain: _____

Halves

1 Shade **half** of each shape:
   a   b

   c   d

2 Shade **half** of each group:
   a   b

   c   d

3 Colour **half** of each picture:
   a   b

   c   d.

4 Draw, then colour **half** of:
   a 8 stars   b 10 diamonds

   c 4 triangles   d 6 circles

5 Shade **half** of the rectangle:

6 Colour **half** of the group:

7 Colour **half** of the television screen:

8 Draw 12 squares and colour **half** of them:

9 Which is bigger $\frac{1}{2}$ or $\frac{3}{4}$? Draw a **picture** to show your answer.

Quarters

1 Shade **1 quarter** of each shape:
   a   b

   c   d

2 Shade **3 quarters** of each shape:
   a   b

   c   d

3 Shade $\frac{1}{4}$ of each group:
   a   b

   c   d

4 Draw, then colour $\frac{3}{4}$ of:
   a 4 stars   b 8 triangles

   c 4 squares   d 12 circles

5 Shade **1 quarter** of the rectangle:

6 Shade **3 quarters** of the square:

7 Shade $\frac{1}{4}$ of:

8 Draw and colour $\frac{3}{4}$ of 8 circles:

9 What is $\frac{1}{4}$ of 8? _____

Eighths

1 What **part of** each shape has been shaded?

a ☐/☐   b ☐/☐

c  ☐/☐   d ☐/☐

2 Colour part of each shape to **match the fraction**:

a $\frac{1}{8}$ b $\frac{7}{8}$

c $\frac{5}{8}$ d $\frac{2}{8}$

3 Colour part of each group to **match the fraction**:

a $\frac{3}{8}$ b $\frac{4}{8}$

c $\frac{5}{8}$ d $\frac{6}{8}$

4 Draw a **diagram or picture** to show:

a $\frac{1}{8}$ of a square   b $\frac{3}{8}$ of a group of 8 circles

c $\frac{5}{8}$ of a group of 8 triangles   d $\frac{6}{8}$ of a rectangle

5 What **part** of the rectangle has been shaded? _____

6 Colour the circle to **match the fraction**: $\frac{3}{8}$

7 Colour the group to show $\frac{2}{8}$.

8 Draw a **diagram/picture** to show: $\frac{7}{8}$ of a set of 8 stars

9 a **Colour** each of the shapes the given fraction.

b What do you **notice**? _____

_____

 $\frac{1}{2}$ $\frac{2}{4}$ $\frac{4}{8}$

Tenths

1 Shade the **fraction** of each rectangle:

a $\frac{3}{10}$ b $\frac{7}{10}$

c $\frac{2}{10}$ d $\frac{8}{10}$

2 Record the shaded **fraction** of each rectangle:

a 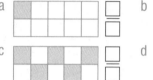 ☐/☐   b ☐/☐

c ☐/☐   d ☐/☐

3 Shade the **fraction** of each group:

a  $\frac{6}{10}$ b $\frac{10}{10}$

c $\frac{3}{10}$ d $\frac{7}{10}$

4 Place each of the fractions on the **number line**:

a $\frac{2}{10}$ b $\frac{8}{10}$ c $\frac{5}{10}$ d $\frac{9}{10}$

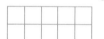

5 Shade the **fraction** of the rectangle:

$\frac{5}{10}$

6 Record the shaded **fraction** of the rectangle:

 ☐/☐

7 Shade the given **fraction** of the group:

$\frac{1}{10}$

8 Place $\frac{3}{10}$ on the **number line**:

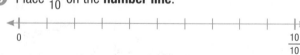

9 Draw a **picture** to show which fraction is bigger:

$\frac{1}{2}$ or $\frac{1}{10}$

See **START UPS** page 6

Naming fractions (3)

1 Write the following fractions as **numbers**:

a one half _____ b three quarters _____

c three eighths _____ d one quarter _____

2 Write the fraction numbers in **words**:

a $\frac{1}{8}$ _____

b $\frac{2}{4}$ _____

c $\frac{1}{2}$ _____

d $\frac{5}{8}$ _____

3 What **part** of each picture has been shaded?

a $\boxed{}$ b  $\boxed{}$

c  $\boxed{}$

d  $\boxed{}$

4 Draw a **picture** to show:

a one half b six eighths

c three quarters d eight eighths

5 Write as a **number**: seven eighths _____

6 Write in **words**: $\frac{5}{8}$ _____

7 What **part** has been shaded?

 $\boxed{}$

8 Draw a **picture** to show: two quarters

9 Write the **fraction** in **words** to describe:

 _____

See **START UPS** page 6

Money – coins

1 Write the **name** of each coin in words:

a _____ b _____

c _____ d  _____

2 Circle the coin of **greatest value** in each set:

a   b

c   d

3 Write the **total** of each set of coins:

a + ⊙ = _____ b ⊙ + ⊙ + ⊙ = _____

c ⊙ + ⊙ + ⊙ = _____

d ⊙ + ⊙ = _____

4 **How many** of each coin is needed to make $1?

a 50c _____ b 20c _____

c 10c _____ d 5c _____

5 Write the **value** of this coin:

 _____

6 Circle the coin of the **greatest value**:

7 Write the **total** of the coins:

⊙ + ⊙ + ⊙ = _____

8 **How many** $1 coins are needed to make one dollar?

_____

9 Circle the **set** of coins of the **greatest value**:

Money – notes

1 Write the **value** of each note:

a   b

_____   _____

c   d

_____   _____

2 Find the **totals** of:

a   +   = ____

b   +   +   = ____

c   +   = ____

d   +   +   +   = ____

3 How many of each note is needed to **make $100**?

a   b

_____   _____

c   d

_____   _____

4 Write how much more would be needed to **make $50**:

a   _____   b   _____

c   _____

d   _____

5 Write the **value** of this note:

 _____

6 Find the **total** of:

 = ____

7 How **many** notes are needed to make

one hundred dollars? ____

8 How much more is needed to **make $50**?

 _____

9 List **three different** combinations of **notes** that could be used to pay for a toy costing $60:

a _____

b _____

c _____

Money

1 Order from **smallest** to **largest** in value:

a   20c, $2, $1, 50c _____

b $1, $50, $20, $10 _____

c $2, $50, 50c, 5c _____

d $1, $10, $50, $2 _____

2 Name the **single coin** that is equal to:

a   5c + 5c = _____

b   10c + 10c = _____

c   50c + 50c = _____

d $1 + 50c + 50c = _____

3 **Match** the price tag with the amounts:

a $1 + $1 + 50c $6.75

b $5 + $2 + 20c + 20c + 5c $2.05

c $5 + $1 + 50c + 20c + 5c $2.50

d $1 + $1 + 5c $7.45

4 Write the **totals**:

a $50 + $20 + $1 + 50c = _____

b $20 + $20 + $2 + $1 + 10c = _____

c $2 + $1 + 50c + 5c = _____

d $2 + 50c + 20c + 10c = _____

5 Order from **smallest to largest**:

50c, 20c, 5c, 10c _____

6 Name the **single coin** that is equal to:

20c + 20c + 10c = _____

7 **Match** the price tag to the amount:
$10 + $1 + 20c + 10c

$1.30 $11.30 $11.03

8 Write the **total**:
$10 + $5 + $1 + 50c + 10c = _____

9 List the **notes and coins** that could be used to buy a DVD costing $12.95.

_____

_____

Patterns with numbers

1 Complete the **number patterns**:

    a 2, 4, 6, 8, ____, ____, ____

    b 10, 20, 30, 40, ____, ____, ____

    c 3, 5, 7, 9, ____, ____, ____

    d 15, 20, 25, 30, ____, ____, ____

2 Find the **missing numbers** in the number patterns:

    a 10, 12, ___, 16, ___, 20

    b 20, 25, ___, 35, ___, 45

    c 100, ___, 80, ___, 60, 50

    d 22, ___, 26, ___, ___, 32

3 Show the **next 5 jumps** of the number pattern on the number line:

    a starting at 2 and counting forwards by 2:

      2

    b starting at 10 and counting forwards by 5:

      10

    c starting at 0 and counting forwards by 10:

      0

    d starting at 30 and counting forwards by 2:

      30

4 Describe the number pattern in **words**:

    a 50, 52, 54, 56, 58 _____

      _____

    b 30, 40, 50, 60, 70 _____

      _____

    c 50, 45, 40, 35, 30 _____

      _____

    d 20, 18, 16, 14, 12 _____

      _____

5 Complete the **number pattern**:

    100, 110, 120, 130, ____, ____, ____, ____

6 Find the **missing numbers**: 30, 28, ___, ___, 22, 20

7 Draw a number line to show the **next 5 jumps** of the number pattern starting at 10 and counting forwards by 2:

      10

8 Describe the number pattern in **words**: 50, 55, 60, 65, 70 _____

9 a Starting at 100 **create a number pattern**. _____

      _____

    b Describe it in **words**. _____

      _____

Patterns with shapes

1 Complete the **patterns**:

    a △, ○, □, △, ○, ____, ____, ____

    b ☆, ☆, ○, ☆, ☆, ____, ____, ____

    c □, □, □, △, △, △, ○, ____, ____, ____

    d □, △, ☆, □, △, ____, ____, ____

2 Describe the patterns in **words**:

    a △, ○, ○, △, ○, ○ _____

    b □, △, ○, □, △, ○ _____

    c ○, ○, □, ○, ○, △, ○, ○, ☆ _____

      _____

    d □, □, □, ○, ○, ○, ☆, ☆, ☆ _____

      _____

3 **Draw** a **pattern** that follows the **rules**:

    a star, circle, star; repeated 2 times

      _____

    b circle, circle, square; repeated 2 times

      _____

    c square, circle, square; repeated 3 times

      _____

    d circle, circle, star; repeated 3 times

      _____

4 Create your **own patterns** and write the **rules**:

    a _____

    b _____

    c _____

    d _____

5 Complete the **pattern**:

    ☆, ☆, ○, ☆, ☆, ○, ____, ____, ____

6 Describe the pattern in **words**:

    ☆, ☆, ○, ☆, ☆, ○ _____

7 Draw a **pattern** that follows the **rule**: circle, square, triangle repeated 3 times _____

8 Create your **own pattern** and write the **rule**:

    _____

9 a Complete the **pattern**: •, ••, •••, ••••, ____, ____, ____

    b What is the **rule**? _____

      _____

Solving problems (addition)

1 Write each as a **number sentence** and solve:

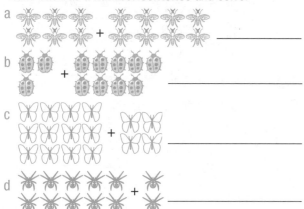

a _____

b _____

c _____

d _____

2 Write each as a **number sentence** and solve:

a   four biscuits add five biscuits _____

b   seven cakes and nine cakes _____

c   eleven sandwiches and seven sandwiches

_____

d   the total of thirteen burgers and six burgers

_____

3 Write a **word problem** for each and solve:

a   12 + 3 = _____

b   15 + 4 = _____

c   7 + 8 = _____

d   6 + 5 = _____

4 Solve each of the **problems**:

a   10 add 5 = ____   b   12 and 7 = ____

c   15 plus 3 = ____   d   20 and 3 more = ____

5 Write as a **number sentence** and solve:

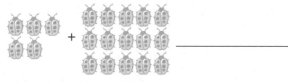 _____

6 Write as a **number sentence** and solve:

six apples and three apples _____

7 Write as a **word problem** and solve:

10 + 0 = _____

8 **Solve**: 11 and 3 more = _____

9 Circle the word that doesn't mean **addition**:

add   subtract   and   plus

Solving problems (subtraction)

1 Write each as a **number sentence** and solve:

a

_____

b

_____

c

_____

d _____

2 Write each as a **number sentence** and solve:

a   the difference between 7 and 2 footballs _____

b   the difference between 11 and 8 tennis balls _____

c   the difference between 10 and 9 golf balls _____

d   the difference between 12 and 5 netballs _____

3 Write a **word problem** for each and solve:

a   10 – 8 = _____

b   9 – 9 = _____

c   12 – 5 = _____

d   19 – 17 = _____

4 Solve each of the **problems**:

a   20 subtract 11 = _____

b   11 take away 5 = _____

c   19 minus 5 = _____

d   the difference between 10 and 2 = _____

5 Write as a **number sentence** and solve:

 _____

6 Write as a **number sentence** and solve:

the difference between 5 and 2 cricket balls _____

7 Write a **word problem** and solve:

18 – 10 = _____

8 **Solve**: 15 take away 12 = _____

9 Circle the fact with the **smaller** answer:

15 – 9   or   16 – 11

2D shapes (1)

1 **Match** the name to the shape:

square rectangle triangle circle rhombus

a _____   b _____

c _____   d _____

2 **Draw** a:

a circle   b triangle

c square   d rectangle

3 Circle the shapes that have **straight sides**:

a   b

c   d

4 **Describe** these shapes in **words**:

a _____

b _____

c _____

d _____

5 **Match** the name to the shape:

square   rectangle

triangle   rhombus

6 **Draw** a square:

7 Does this shape have **straight sides**? _____

8 **Describe** the shape in **words**: _____

9 Draw a **6 sided shape**:

2D shapes (2)

1 Count the **number of sides** for each shape:

a _____   b _____

c _____   d _____

2 Count the **number of corners** for each shape:

a _____   b _____

c _____   d _____

3 Circle the shapes that are **triangles**:

a   b

c   d

4 Which of the shapes have:

A   B   C   D

E   F   G

a 4 **sides**? _____ b **equal sides**? _____

c 6 **sides**? _____ d 3 **sides**? _____

5 Count the number of **sides**: ____

6 Count the number of **corners**: ____

7 Is this shape a **triangle**? _____

8 Which of the shapes has **equal sides**? _____

A   B   C

9 Write a 'Who am I?' for a **rhombus**:

_____

_____

_____

Squares and rectangles

1 Circle the shape that is a **square**:

a   b

c   d

2 **Draw** a:

a   square   b   rectangle

c   triangle   d   circle

3 How many **sides** have:

a   2 squares? _____

b   3 rectangles? _____

c   2 rectangles? _____

d   3 squares? _____

4 How many **corners** have:

a   2 rectangles? _____

b   3 rectangles? _____

c   2 squares? _____

d   3 squares? _____

5 Circle the shape that is a **square**:

6 **Draw** 2 triangles.

7 How many **sides** have 5 rectangles? _____

8 How many **corners** have 4 squares? _____

9 How many of the following **features** does a **square** have?

a   straight lines _____

b   curved lines _____

c   sides _____

d   corners _____

Kites, rombuses and circles

1 **Draw** a:

a   square   b   kite

c   rhombus   d   circle

2 How many **sides** has a:

a   circle? _____

b   kite? _____

c   rectangle? _____

d   rhombus? _____

3 Circle the **rhombus**:

a   b

c   d

4 How many **corners** has a:

a   rhombus? _____

b   kite? _____

c   circle? _____

d   rectangle? _____

5 **Draw** a rectangle:

6 How many **sides** does a square have? _____

7 Circle the **rhombus**:

8 How many **corners** does a square have? _____

9 On the dot paper draw **2 different kites**:

3D objects (1)

1 Name the **shape** of each of the shaded faces:

a   b   c   d

_____   _____   _____   _____

2 How many of each of the **3D objects** can you see in the picture?

a   b   c   d

_____   _____   _____

3 Draw a line matching the **3D object** to its name:

a sphere   b cube   c prism   d cylinder

4 How many **faces** does each 3D object have?

a   b   c   d

_____   _____   _____   _____

5 Name the **shape** of the shaded face:

  _____

6 How many **cubes** can you see in the picture below?

  _____

7 Draw a line matching the **3D object** to its name:

a rectangular prism   b triangular prism   c cube

8 How many **surfaces** does have? _____

9 **What am I?**

I have one curved surface and 2 flat surfaces.

These flat surfaces are circles.

I am a _____

3D objects (2)

1 How many **faces** does each 3D object have?

a   b

_____   _____

c   d

_____   _____

2 How many **corners** does each 3D object have?

a cube ____

b rectangular prism ____

c pyramid ____

d sphere ____

3 How many **edges** does each 3D object have?

a   b

_____   _____

c   d

_____   _____

4 Draw what you would see if you looked at this **3D object from above**:

a   b

_____   _____

c   d

_____   _____

5 How many **faces** does have? _____

6 How many **corners** does a triangular prism have? _____

7 How many **edges** does have? _____

8 Draw what you would see if you looked at the sphere **from above**:

_____

9 Write a '**What am I?**' for this pyramid:

_____

_____

_____

Length informal (1)

1 Circle the **longest** object:

a

b

c   d

2 Circle the **shortest** object:

a   b

c   d

3 Using your finger width, measure the **length** of the following:

a ▢   _____

b ▢   _____

c ▢   _____

d ▢

_____

4 Match the **object** and the **tool** to measure it:

a   b   c   d

5 Circle the **longest** object:

6 Circle the **shortest** person:

7 Using your finger width, measure the **length** of: ____

8 Match the **object** to the **tool** used to measure it:

     ▦

9 Order the following items from **shortest** (1) to **longest** (4):

Crocodile   Fish   Crab   Whale

____   ____   ____   ____

Length informal (2)

1 Circle the **shortest** object:

a carrot
b pea
c bunch of celery
d potato

2 Compare the crayons and circle the **shortest**:

a
b
c
d

3 Estimate the **length** of each object in handspans:

a a girl's foot _____
b a man's arm _____
c a boy's leg _____
d a school desk _____

4 Match the **object** with the **tool** to measure it:

a curvy line   finger
b length of texta   handspan
c height of a dog   string
d matchbox   ruler

5 Circle the **shortest** object:

table,   chair,   book

6 Compare the crayons and circle the **longest**:

7 Estimate the **length** of your step in handspans: _____

8 What **tool** would be used to measure the line around Australia on a map?

A ruler or string? _____

9 Estimate the **length** of each side of the rectangle using your finger width: _____

Comparing length

1. Order the lengths from **shortest** (1) to **longest** (4):

2. Order the following from **shortest** (1) to **longest** (4):

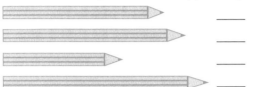

3. Order the lengths from **shortest** (1) to **longest** (4):

4. Order the lengths from **shortest** (1) to **longest** (4):

5. Order the lengths from **shorter** (1) to **longer** (2):

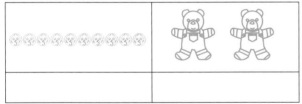

6. Order the following from **shorter** (1) to **longer** (2):

7. Order the lengths from **shorter** (1) to **longer** (2):

8. Order the lengths from **shorter** (1) to **longer** (2):

9. If you measured something **10 counters long**, what might the object be?

   Give 3 ideas:

   _____ _____ _____

Area (1)

1. Circle the object with the **smallest area**:

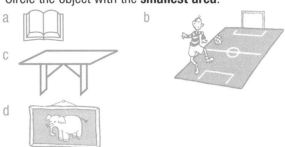

2. Circle the object with the **largest area**:

3. Estimate the **areas** of the following using the palm of your hand:
   a a book _____ palms   b the table top _____ palms
   c seat of a chair ____ palms
   d a coin _____ palms

4. Match the **method** you would use to measure the area of:
   a a leaf   palm of hand
   b calculator   a stone
   c floor of a classroom   a counter
   d pencil case   newspaper sheets

5. Circle the object with the **smaller area**:

6. Circle the object with the **larger area**:

7. Estimate the **area** of a poster or picture using the palm of your hand: _____

8. Circle the object you would use to **measure the area** of a cupboard door:

   stone   newspaper sheets

9. Which object has the **largest area** and why?

Area (2)

1 Find the **area** of the shapes in squares:

a  _____　　　b _____

c _____　　　d _____

2 Estimate the **area** of the following:

a _____　　　b _____

c _____　　　d  _____

3 Find the **area** of each shape:

a ____ squares　　　b ____ squares

c ____ squares　　　d ____ squares

4 Draw **4 different** shapes (a – d) of **6 squares**:

5 Find the **area** of:  ____ squares

6 Estimate the **area** of: ____ squares

7 Find the **area** of this shape: ____ squares

8 Draw a shape that has the area of **4 squares**:

9 Draw a shape with a **larger area**:

Comparing area

1 Order the areas from **smallest** (1) to **largest** (4):

_____　_____　_____　_____

2 Order the areas from **smallest** (1) to **largest** (4):

_____

3 Order the areas from **smallest** (1) to **largest** (4):

4 Order the areas from **smallest** (1) to **largest** (4):

5 Order the areas from **smaller** (1) to **larger** (2):

 ____　　　 ____

6 Order the areas from **smaller** (1) to **larger** (2):

 ____　　　 ____

7 Order the areas from **smaller** (1) to **larger** (2):

8 Order the areas from **smaller** (1) to **larger** (2):

_____　　　_____

9 If you found the **area** of an object to be 10 counters, what might that object be? **Give 3 ideas**:

_____

_____

_____

Capacity informal

1 Order the measuring equipment from **smallest** (1) to **largest** (4) in capacity:

 ____ ____ ____ ____

2 Circle the object with the **greatest capacity** in each pair:

a

b

c

d

3 Which containers would be best to measure the **capacity** of each object:

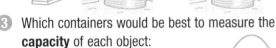

A   B   C

a b c d

4 Ashley used a cup to fill different containers with water.

a Which container holds the **most** water? ____

Container	Number of cups needed
A	
B	
C	
D	

b Which container holds the **least** water? ____

c How many cups did **container D** hold? ____

d Which container holds **3 cups** of water? ____

5 Order the measuring equipment from **smaller** (1) to **larger** (2) capacity:

 ____ ____

6 Circle the object with the **greater capacity**:

7 Match the container which would be best to measure the **capacity** of: A   B

C

8 In Q4, how many cups did **container A** hold? _____

9 A big problem! How could you measure the **amount of water** in a swimming pool?

_____

_____

Cubic centimetres

1 How many **cubes** are in each model?

a   b

____   ____

c   d

____   ____

2 How many **cubes** are in these models?

a   b

____   ____

c   d

____   ____

3 Order the models from Question 2 from **smallest** (1) to **largest** (4):

a ____   b ____   c ____   d ____

4 Circle the **smallest** model in each pair:

a  b

c   d

5 How many **cubes** are in the model? ____

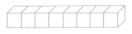

6 How many **cubes** are in this model? ____

7 Order the models from **smaller** (1) to **larger** (3).

 ____ ____  ____

8 Circle the **larger** model in the pair:

9 Colour **10 cubic blocks** in this model:

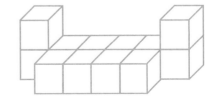

Ordering volume

1 Record the **volumes** by counting the number of cubes in each:

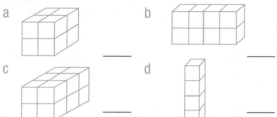

a ＿＿＿＿　b ＿＿＿＿

c ＿＿＿＿　d ＿＿＿＿

2 Order the models in Question 1 from **smallest** (1) to **largest** (3) volume:

a ＿＿＿＿　　　b ＿＿＿＿

c ＿＿＿＿　　　d ＿＿＿＿

3 Record the **volume** of water in each object:

a ＿＿＿＿＿　b ＿＿＿＿＿

c ＿＿＿＿＿　d ＿＿＿＿＿

4 Order the volumes in Question 3 from **smallest** (1) to **largest** (4):

a ＿＿＿＿　　　b ＿＿＿＿

c ＿＿＿＿　　　d ＿＿＿＿

5 Record the **volume**: ＿＿＿＿

6 Circle the object with the **largest volume**:

7 Record the **volume**: ＿＿＿＿＿

8 Circle the object with the **larger volume**:

9 Max put 50 L of petrol in his car and 30 L in his daughter's car. **How many litres** of petrol altogether?

＿＿＿＿＿＿＿＿＿＿＿＿＿＿＿＿＿＿＿＿

Mass informal (1)

1 Complete the following sentences:

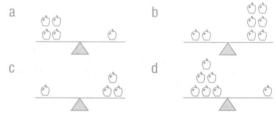

a The watermelon **weighs** ＿＿＿＿ than 1 kg.

b The lollies **weigh** ＿＿＿＿ than 1 kg.

c The apples **weigh** ＿＿＿＿＿ than 1 kg.

d The oranges **weigh** ＿＿＿＿＿ than 1 kg.

2 Circle the **heavier** object in each **pair**:

a feather　　　　　brick

b football　　　　　television

c a pencil case　　pile of books

d tennis ball　　　bag of apples

3 Draw the **extra apples** needed to make the scales balance:

a　　　　　　　　b

c　　　　　　　　d

4 Answer the questions:

A　　　　　B　　　　　C

a What is **heavier than** the bananas? ＿＿＿＿＿

b What is **lighter than** the apples? ＿＿＿＿＿

c What 2 items are the **same weight**? ＿＿＿＿＿

d What is **lighter than** the watermelon? ＿＿＿＿＿

5 Complete the sentence: The corn **weighs** ＿＿＿＿ than 1 kg.

6 Circle the **heavier** object:

potato　　　grapes

7 Draw the **extra apples** needed to make the scales balance:

8 What is **heavier than** the strawberries (in Question 4)?

9 What is **heavier**; 2 potatoes or 1 watermelon?

＿＿＿＿＿＿＿＿＿＿＿＿＿＿＿＿＿＿＿＿

How do you know? ＿＿＿＿＿＿＿＿＿＿＿

＿＿＿＿＿＿＿＿＿＿＿＿＿＿＿＿＿＿＿＿

UNIT 95
See START UPS page 7

Mass informal (2)

1 Order the objects from **lightest** (1) to **heaviest** (4).

____   ____   ____   ____

2 Order the animals from **heaviest** (1) to **lightest** (4).

elephant   horse   spider   bird

____   ____   ____   ____

3 Complete the scales to match the sentences:

a the elephant is **heavier** than the cat:

b 1 apple is the **same weight** as 1 orange:

c the dog is **heavier** than the snake:

d the mouse is **lighter** than the cat:

4 If 1 apple = 5 strawberries, **balance** the scales:

a    b

c    d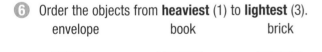

5 Order the objects from **lightest** (1) to **heaviest** (3).

football   ping pong ball   tennis ball

____   ____   ____

6 Order the objects from **heaviest** (1) to **lightest** (3).

envelope   book   brick

____   ____   ____

7 Complete the scales to show that an ant is **lighter** than a spider:

8 If 1 apple = 5 strawberries **balance** the scales:

9 Name 4 things that are **heavier** than you!

_____

_____

_____

UNIT 96
See START UPS page 7

Time analogue (hour)

1 Draw in the **hour hand** to complete the times:

a 4 o'clock   b 7 o'clock

c 1 o'clock   d 11 o'clock

2 **Write the time** shown on each clock face:

a   b

_____   _____

c   d

_____   _____

3 **Draw the time** given on each clock:

a 3 o'clock   b 10 o'clock

c 9 o'clock   d 6 o'clock

4 Order the times from **earliest** (1) to **latest** (4):

4 o'clock   2 o'clock   10 o'clock   7 o'clock

____   ____   ____   ____

5 Draw the **hour hand** to complete the time: 3 o'clock

6 **Write the time**: _____

7 **Draw the time** 5 o'clock.

8 Order the times from **earliest** (1) to **latest** (3):

11 o'clock   2 o'clock   7 o'clock

____   ____   ____

9 How many **minutes** are in 1 **hour**? _____

Time analogue (half hour)

1 Draw the **hour hand** to complete the times:

a half past 3   b half past 7

c half past 11   d half past 4

2 **Write the time** shown on each clock face:

a _____   b _____

c _____   d _____

3 **Draw the time** given on each clock face:

a half past 5   b half past 12

c half past 8   d half past 1

4 Order the following times from **earliest** (1) to **latest** (4).

half past 6   half past 9   half past 2   half past 8

____   ____   ____   ____

5 Draw the **hour hand** to show the time, half past 10.

6 **Write the time** shown on the clock. _____

7 **Draw half past 8** on the clock.

8 Order the times from **earliest** (1) to **latest** (3):

half past 7   half past 5   half past 6

____   ____   ____

9 How many **minutes** are there in **half an hour**? _____

Time analogue (quarter past)

1 Draw the **time** given on each clock face:

a quarter past 3   b quarter past 7   c quarter past 1   d quarter past 10

2 **Write the time** shown:

a _____   b _____

c _____   d _____

3 **Draw the hands** on the watches to show the time:

a quarter past 6   b quarter past 2   c 4 o'clock   d half past 9

4 Match the **times** with the **clock faces**:

a quarter past 7   b quarter past 4   c quarter past 2   d quarter past 11

5 Draw **quarter past 9** on the clock face.

6 **Write the time** shown: _____

7 Draw **half past 2** on the watch.

8 Match the **times** with the **clock faces**:

a quarter past 5   b quarter past 6   c quarter past 3

9 If school finishes at a quarter past 3, and football practice doesn't start until half past 5, **how long** does Alex have to wait? _____

Analogue time (quarter to)

1 How many **minutes** are in:

a 1 hour? _____   b a quarter of an hour? _____

c half an hour? _____   d 2 hours? _____

2 On each clock face **draw the time** given:

a quarter to 3   b quarter to 9

c quarter to 1   d quarter to 12

3 **Write the time** shown on each clock face:

a _____   b _____

c  _____   d _____

4 **Draw the time** given on each of the clock faces:

a quarter **to** 5    b quarter **past** 2

c quarter **to** 10   d quarter **past** 7

5 How many **minutes** are in 3 hours? _____

6 **Draw the time**; quarter to 8:

7 Write the **time shown**:

_____

_____

8 **Draw the time**; quarter past 6.

9 How many **minutes** does it take the hour hand to move from one number to the next? _____

Digital time (1)

1 Match the **digital times** with the **words**:

a one thirty   11:00

b eight forty five   3:15

c eleven o'clock   1:30

d three fifteen   8:45

2 Write the following digital times with **numbers**:

a six fifteen _____

b nine thirty _____

c four o'clock _____

d seven forty-five _____

3 Write the following times in **words**:

a 10:15 _____

b 2:00 _____

c 12:45 _____

d 5:30 _____

4 **Complete** the labels:

a 8:30   b 5:45

____ past ____   quarter to ____

c 3:00   d 2:15

____ o'clock   quarter past ____

5 **Match**: six forty-five

9:15   3:30   6:45

6 Write seven fifteen in **numbers**. _____

7 Write 1:30 in **words**. _____

8 **Complete**: 10:30 ____ past ____

9 **Match** the times:

a 3:15   b 7:30   c 9:45

Digital time (2)

1 **Write the time** on the digital clocks:

　a　quarter to 3　　　b　half past 6

　[:]　　　　　[:]

　c　9 o'clock　　　d　quarter past 10

　[:]　　　　　[:]

2 Complete the **labels**:

　a　[1 : 15]　　　b　[12 : 00]

　quarter past ____　　____ o'clock

　c　[8 : 45]　　　d　[4 : 30]

　quarter to ____　　____ past ____

3 **Match** the **times**:

　a　half past 11　　　[7 : 45]

　b　5 o'clock　　　　[2 : 15]

　c　quarter to 8　　　[11 : 30]

　d　quarter past 2　　[5 : 00]

4 Write the times in **words**:

　a　7:15 _____

　b　9:00 _____

　c　1:30 _____

　d　3:00 _____

5 **Write** a quarter past 4 on the digital clock. [:]

6 Complete the **label**: _____ past _____ [7 : 30]

7 **Match** the correct **time**:　quarter to 1

　　　　　　　　　　　quarter to 2　[1 : 45]

　　　　　　　　　　　quarter past 1

8 Write 5:00 in **words**. _____

9 Write and draw the times you **start and finish** school each day:

| Start | [:] | |
| Finish | [:] | |

Months

1 Circle the names of **months**:

　a　May

　b　Mars

　c　November

　d　Wednesday

2 Circle the **month** which is the first one of the year:

　a　July

　b　June

　c　January

　d　December

3 Circle the **month** which is the last one of the year:

　a　October

　b　August

　c　December

　d　April

4 Expand the **abbreviated month** names:

　a　Jan _____

　b　Oct _____

　c　Sept _____

　d　Dec _____

5 Circle the name of a **month**:

　August　　　Thursday　　　Pluto

6 Circle the month which is **before** June:

　May　　　August　　　July

7 Circle the month which is **after** August:

　July　　　September　　　January

8 Expand the **abbreviated month** name:
Nov _____

9 a　How many **months** in a year? _____

　b　List the **months of the year** in order.

　_____　_____　_____

　_____　_____　_____

　_____　_____　_____

　_____　_____　_____

Seasons

1. Circle names which are **seasons**:
   a Festival
   b Spring
   c Autumn
   d Summer

2. Circle the months which are in **Spring**:
   a December
   b November
   c January
   d September

3. Circle the months which are in **Winter**:
   a June
   b September
   c February
   d July

4. Circle the **hottest months** of the year:
   a January
   b September
   c July
   d February

5. Circle names which are **seasons**:

   Water   Winter   Mars

6. Circle the months which are in **Spring**:

   June   October   February

7. Circle the months which are in **Winter**:

   August   April   December

8. Circle the **coldest months** of the year:

   January   June   July

9. Investigate when the **wet season** and the **dry season** occur in tropical areas.

   _____

   _____

   _____

The Calendar

1. How many:
   a **months** in a year? _____
   b **days** in one week? _____
   c **days** in a fortnight (2 weeks)? _____
   d **days** in January? _____

2. On which **day of the week** are the dates:
   a 12th September?
   b 20th September?
   c 30th September?
   d 1st September?

   | September | | | | | | |
S	M	T	W	Th	F	S
	1	2	3	4	5	6	7
8	9	10	11	12	13	14
15	16	17	18	19	20	21
22	23	24	25	26	27	28
29	30					

3. Circle the **months** which have 31 days:
   a March
   b November
   c June
   d August

4. Which **date** is:
   a the first Sunday?
   b the last Tuesday?
   c the 2nd Monday?
   d the 3rd Wednesday?

   | July | | | | | | |
S	M	T	W	Th	F	S
		1	2	3	4	5	6
7	8	9	10	11	12	13
14	15	16	17	18	19	20
21	22	23	24	25	26	27
28	29	30	31			

5. How many **days** in December? _____

6. Looking at the calendar in Question 2, on which **day** is the 11th September?

   _____

7. Circle the **months** that have 30 days:

   April   February   September

8. Looking at the calendar in Question 4, which **date** is the 2nd Friday of the month of July?

   _____

9. Write the **number of days** for each of the months in Spring.

   _____

Position

1 The picture shows pencil boxes on shelves. Whose pencil box is:

a on the top shelf in the **middle**? _____

b on the bottom shelf on the **left**? _____

c on the 2nd shelf on the **right**? _____

d **below** Alex's pencil box? _____

2 Describe the **position** of:

a Alex's pencil box. _____

b Veronica's pencil box. _____

c Sarah's pencil box. _____

d Tom's pencil box. _____

3 At the tuckshop, what food item is:

a on the top shelf to the **right**? _____

b in the **middle**? _____

c on the bottom shelf to the **left**? _____

d **above** the sandwich? _____

4 Describe the **position** of the:

a orange juice _____

b orange _____

c sandwich _____

d water bottle _____

5 Whose pencil box is in the **middle** in Question 1?

_____

6 Describe the **position** of Beth's pencil box in Question 1.

_____

7 What food item is on the **middle shelf to the right** in Question 3?

_____

8 Describe the **position** of all the drinks.

_____

9 Pick 3 lunch items from Question 3 and describe the **position** of these items.

_____

_____

_____

Position – giving directions

1 In this house:

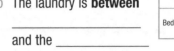

a Bedroom 3 is **next to** _____

b The laundry is **between** _____ and the _____

c The kitchen is **next to** the _____

d The bathroom is **near** the _____

2 **Complete**:

a from Bedroom 3 to the bathroom you will pass

_____

b from Bedroom 1 to the kitchen you will pass

_____

c from Bedroom 1 to Bedroom 3 you will pass

_____

d from the laundry to the kitchen you will pass

_____

3 On this map, using the words up, down, right and left, **give directions** from:

a A to F _____

_____

b C to G _____

c B to D _____

d F to C _____

4 Look at the grid. Start at A and give **directions** to:

a B _____

b C _____

c D _____

d E _____

	B		F
		C	
			D
A	E		

5 Look at the house from Question 1. Bedroom 2 is **between** _____

6 **Complete**: To get from Bedroom 2 to the Bathroom you will pass _____

7 Use the map from Question 3 to give **directions** from E to G. _____

8 Look at the grid from Question 4. Start at A and give **directions** to F. _____

9 On a piece of paper draw a map of your house and give **3 sets of directions** from your bedroom to other rooms in your house.

Maps

1 Use the **grid** to find the symbol at:

a A1 _____

b C3 _____

c B3 _____

d D2 _____

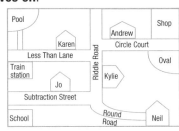

2 Give the **grid reference** for the symbols:

a + _____　　　b ⬜ _____

c ◆ _____　　　d @ _____

3 **Who lives on**:

a Subtraction Street?　　b Less Than Lane?

_____　　　_____

c Riddle Road?　　　d Round Road?

_____　　　_____

4 Describe **the position** of the:

a shop _____

_____

b school _____

_____

c pool _____

_____

d oval _____

_____

5 Use the **grid** from Question 1 to find the symbol at C4:

_____

6 Give the **grid reference** for the ○ in Question 1: _____

7 **Who lives at** Circle Court in Question 3? _____

8 Describe the **position** of the train station:

_____

9 **Create a grid** to show the following pictures and positions:

% A1　　　⬜ A3

≈ B2　　　▲ B4

○ C1　　　■ C3

```
4
3
2
1
  A  B  C
```

Transformations (slide)

1 **Slide** the shape in the direction of the arrow and draw it in the new position:

a →　　　b

c ← 　　　d

2 **Slide** each of the shapes to the **right**:

a →　　　b

c 　　　d

3 Colour the grid to show the shapes **slid to the left**:

a 　　　b

c 　　　d

4 Describe the **slide** of the shape:

a _____

b  _____

c _____

d 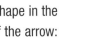 _____

5 **Slide** the shape in the direction of the arrow:

6 **Slide** the shape to the **right**:

7 Colour the grid to show the shape **slid to the left**:

8 Describe the **slide** of the shape: _____

9 Complete the pattern by **sliding** the triangles down and right:

Transformations (flip)

1 **Flip** the shapes to the right:

a   b

c   d

2 **Flip** the shapes down:

a   b   c   d

3 Complete the patterns by **flipping tiles** to the right:

a   b

c   d

4 Describe each of the **flips**:

a _____

b _____

c _____

d _____

5 **Flip** the shape to the right:

6 **Flip** the shape down:

7 Complete the pattern by **flipping the tiles** to the right:

8 Describe the **flip**:
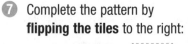
_____

9 Complete the picture by **flipping**:

Transformations (quarter turn)

1 Turn the square **a quarter turn** to the right:

a   b

c   d

2 Turn the triangle **a quarter turn** to the right:

a   b

c   d

3 Turn the square **a quarter turn** to the left:

a   b

c   d

4 If the spinner was turned **a quarter turn** to the right, colour the correct piece:

a   b

c   d

5 Turn the rectangle **a quarter turn** to the right:

6 Turn the triangle **a quarter turn** to the right:

7 Turn the rectangle **a quarter turn** to the left:

8 If the spinner was turned **a quarter turn** to the right, colour the correct piece:

9 Complete the pattern by **turning** the tiles:

UNIT 111

See **START UPS** page 8

Transformations (half turn)

1. Turn the square **a half turn** to the right:

a   b

c   d

2. Turn the triangle **a half turn** to the right:

a   b

c   d

3. If the spinner was turned **a half turn** to the right, colour the correct piece:

a   b

c   d

4. Describe each of the **turns**:

a _____

b _____

c _____

d _____

5. Turn the rectangle **a half turn** to the right:

6. Turn the triangle **a half turn** to the right:

7. If the spinner was turned **a half turn** to the right, colour the correct piece:

8. Describe the **turn**:
 _____

9. **Turn** the book across the table three more times:

MATHS

MATHS

UNIT 112

See **START UPS** page 8

Angles

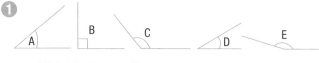

A B C D E

1.
a Which is the **smallest** angle? _____
b Which is the **largest** angle? _____
c Which is the **right** angle? _____
d Is angle A **smaller than** angle C? _____

2. Circle the **right angles**:

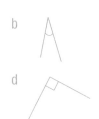

a   b

c   d

3. Circle the angles which are **larger** than a right angle:

a   b

c   d

4. On these clock faces:

A   B   C   D

a which clock hands make the **smallest** angle? _____
b which clock hands make the **largest** angle? _____
c which clock hands make the **same** angle? _____
d which clock hands make a **right** angle? _____

5. Is **larger than** ? _____

6. Is a **right angle**? _____

7. Is  **larger than** a right angle? _____

8. A B Which clock hands make the **larger angle**? _____

9. **How many angles** can you see in this shape?

 _____

☞ Answers on page 96   Units   **65**

Chance

1 Match one of the words from the list to match the statements:
likely, unlikely, certain, impossible
a I will fly to the moon tomorrow. _____
b I will have school holidays this year. _____
c Friday will come after Thursday. _____
d I will become Prime Minister. _____

2 If I roll a die, use the words **possible** or **impossible** to describe the **chance** of:
a rolling a 2 _____
b rolling a 6 _____
c rolling a 0 _____
d rolling a 10 _____

3 On the spinner:
a how many **different outcomes** are possible?
_____
b which section is the spinner **most likely** to land on? _____
c which section is the spinner **least likely** to land on? _____
d Is the spinner **more likely** to land on ⠿ than ≡?
_____

4 Write an example of an event for each of the chance words:
a **likely** _____
b **unlikely** _____
c **certain** _____
d **impossible** _____

5 Match one of the words from the list to describe the statement: **likely, unlikely, certain, impossible**

The sun will set today. _____

6 If I roll a die, what is the chance of a 1 being rolled?

_____ (**possible** or **impossible**)

7 For the spinner in Question 3, is ⠿ **more likely** to be selected than ◢? _____

8 Write an example of a **possible** event.

_____

9 List **3 different** games that involve chance.

_____ _____ _____

Organising data

1 A coin was tossed and here are the results.
(H = heads, T = tails)
H, T, T, H, H, H, H, T, H, T,
H, T, T, T, H, H, H, H, H, T
Complete the **table**:

		Tally	Total
Heads	a	_____	b _____
Tails	c	_____	d _____

2 Here are the numbers rolled on one die.
1, 3, 4, 6, 2, 3, 5,
6, 1, 3, 2, 3, 3, 6,
5, 4, 1, 3, 2, 5, 6,
6, 3, 3, 4
Complete the **table**:

		Tally	Total
a	1		
b	2		
	3	ǁǁǁ ǁǁǁ	8
c	4		
d	5		
	6	ǁǁǁ	5

3 Here are some shapes collected by students.
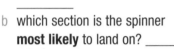

	Tally	Total
△	ǁǁǁ ǀ	a _____
○	b _____	c _____
□	ǁǁǁ ǀ	d _____

Complete the **table**:

4 Here is a **tally sheet** which records the number of cars families have.

0	ǁǁǁ
1	ǁǁǁ ǁǁǀ
2	ǁǁǁ ǁǁǁ ǁǀ
3	ǁǀǀ

a What is the **most common** number of cars? ____
b What is the **least common** number of cars? ____
c **How many** families have no cars? ____
d **How many** families have 1 car? ____

5 Using question 1: **How many** times was the coin tossed? _____

6 Using question 2: **How many** times was the die rolled? _____

7 Using question 3: **How many** shapes were collected? _____

8 Using question 4: **How many** families were asked about cars? ____

9 Here is a collection of data. Create your own **tally sheet**:

Picture graphs

① Gemma made the graph of the number of shapes she collected.

a What shape did Gemma have the **most** of? _____

b What shape did Gemma have the **least** of? _____

c **How many** circles did Gemma have? _____

d **How many** triangles did Gemma have? _____

② This is a graph of 2C's favourite fruit.

a What is the **most popular** fruit? _____

b What is the **least popular** fruit? _____

c **How many** students liked watermelon? _____

d **How many** students liked oranges? _____

③ Grace collected information about people's favourite sport. Use the information to complete the **picture graph**:

football	‖‖‖ ‖	7
soccer	‖‖‖	4
netball	‖‖‖ ‖	6
dancing	‖‖‖	3

④ Using the information from Question 3:

a What was the **most popular** sport? _____

b What was the **least popular** sport? _____

c **How many** people preferred soccer? _____

d **How many** people preferred netball? _____

⑤ In Question 1, **how many** shapes did Gemma collect altogether? _____

⑥ In Question 2, **how many** students are in 2C? _____

⑦ In Question 3, **how many** people were surveyed? _____

⑧ In Question 3, **how many more** people preferred football to dancing? _____

⑨ Using the data: H, T, H, T, T, T, H, H, T, H,
T, H, T, T, T, H, T, H, T, T

a create a **tally table**   b create a **picture graph**

Reading data

① Here are the results of rolling a die.

1	‖‖‖
2	‖‖‖‖
3	‖‖‖‖
4	‖‖‖‖ ‖
5	‖‖‖‖
6	‖

a What number was rolled the **most**? _____

b What number was rolled the **least**? _____

c What number was rolled **5 times**? _____

d What numbers were rolled an **equal number** of times? _____

② Here is a tick sheet of the number of coloured cars driving past.

red	✔✔✔✔
blue	✔✔✔✔✔ ✔✔
green	✔✔✔
white	✔✔✔✔
black	✔✔✔✔✔ ✔

a What was the **most common** colour? _____

b What was the **least common** colour? _____

c What colour appeared **6 times**? _____

d What colour appeared **5 times**? _____

③ Here is a table of the number of pieces of equipment in 2F's classroom.

Scissors	Pens	Glue	Erasers	Rulers
12	30	17	15	20

a Which is the **least** number of items? _____

b Which is the **most** number of items? _____

c **Which item** has 20 pieces? _____

d **Which item** has 17 pieces? _____

④ Here is a graph of animals seen in the nature park.

a Which animal was seen the **most**? _____

b Which animal was seen the **least**? _____

c Which animal was seen **4 times**? _____

d Which animal was seen **6 times**? _____

⑤ In Question 1, what was the **total number** of rolls for the numbers 1, 2 and 3? _____

⑥ In Question 2, what coloured cars appeared the **same number** of times? _____

⑦ In Question 3, **how many** pens and rulers as in 2F's classroom? _____

⑧ In Question 4, what was the **total number** of animals seen? _____

⑨ Looking at Questions 1 – 4, which method of **recording data** do you prefer and why? _____

_____

_____

Addition practice

1 Write and solve the **number sentences** for:

a 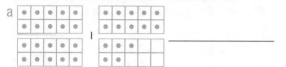 | _____

b  + _____

c  + _____

d + _____

2 **Complete**:

a
T	U
7	1
+ 1	4

b
T	U
6	3
+ 2	5

c
T	U
4	3
+ 2	6

d
T	U
1	1
+ 4	7

3 Find the **total number** of:

a 23 cats and 15 dogs _____

b 26 frogs and 41 lizards _____

c 43 snakes and 12 crocodiles _____

d 51 spiders and 17 butterflies _____

4 **Solve** the following:

a 33 + 42 = _____

b 47 + 51 = _____

c 24 + 43 = _____

d 62 + 33 = _____

5 Write and solve the **number sentence** for:

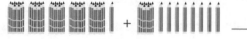 + _____

6 **Complete**:
T	U
4	3
+ 3	5

7 Find the **total number** of 17 lions and 42 tigers. _____

8 **Solve**: 53 + 24 = _____

9 Find the **total** of: 52 + 31 + 16 = _____

Subtraction practice

1 Use **open number lines** to find:

a 27 − 14 =

b 38 − 12 =

c 46 − 21 =

d 56 − 43 =

2 Find:

a the **difference** between 20 and 12 _____

b 27 **minus** 14 _____

c 45 **less** 23 _____

d 56 **takeaway** 26 _____

3 **Complete**:

a
T	U
6	8
− 2	4

b
T	U
7	7
− 4	6

c
T	U
5	9
− 5	1

d
T	U
8	5
− 6	2

4 Find the **missing numbers**:

a
```
    7  9
 − □  3
 ──────
    2 □
```

b
```
    8  8
 − □  8
 ──────
    3 □
```

c
```
    9  6
 − 4 □
 ──────
  □  1
```

d
```
    6 □
 − 2  3
 ──────
  □  4
```

5 Use the **open number line** to find: 38 − 23 = _____

6 Find the **difference** between 73 and 51. _____

7 **Complete**:
T	U
5	3
− 3	1

8 Find the **missing numbers**:
```
    8  6
 − □  2
 ──────
    7 □
```

9 **Check** Hugo's answer to: 79 − 47 = 32

_____

Excel Start Up Maths Year 2   ☞ Answers on page 97

Multiplication practice

1 Write a **number sentence** and solve it for each diagram:

a ○○○   ○○○   ○○○   b
  ○○   ○○   ○○

_____   _____

c | x x | x x | x x | x x | d

_____   _____

2 Write a **number sentence** and solve it for:

a 7 **groups of** 3 turtles _____

b 9 **groups of** 6 fish _____

c 10 **groups of** 3 dolphins _____

d 4 **groups of** 6 crabs _____

3 Complete:

a $4 \times 9 =$ _____   b $8 \times 1 =$ _____

c   7   d   1 0
   $\times$ 6 $\times$ 3

4 Complete:

a
$\times$	1	2	3	4
5				

b
$\times$	4	5	6	7
8				

c
$\times$	2	4	6	8
9				

d
$\times$	3	5	7	9
3				

5 Write a **number sentence** and solve it for:

the number of legs on 6 insects: _____

6 Write a **number sentence** and solve it for:

6 groups of 8 seagulls _____

7 Complete   9
            $\times$ 7

8 Complete
$\times$	4	7	3	8
4				

9 If there are 9 cakes in a packet,
how many cakes are in 9 packets?

_____

Division practice

1 Complete:

a 18 **shared between** 3 = _____

b 12 **shared between** 6 = _____

c 25 **shared between** 5 = _____

d 10 **shared between** 10 = _____

2 Complete:

a $4 \times 6 = 24$ $24 \div 4 =$ _____ $24 \div 6 =$ _____

b $7 \times 3 = 21$ $21 \div 7 =$ _____ $21 \div 3 =$ _____

c $6 \times 7 = 42$ $42 \div 6 =$ _____ $42 \div 7 =$ _____

d $5 \times 10 = 50$ $50 \div 5 =$ _____ $50 \div 10 =$ _____

3 Complete:

a $30 \div 3 =$ _____

b $27 \div 9 =$ _____

c $40 \div 4 =$ _____

d $90 \div 10 =$ _____

4 How **many groups** of:

a 5 cows in 21? ___ r ___

b 3 horses in 20? ___ r ___

c 6 goats in 20? ___ r ___

d 8 sheep in 30? ___ r ___

5 Complete: 60 **shared between** 6 = _____ each

6 Complete:

$4 \times 8 = 32$ $32 \div 4 =$ _____ $32 \div 8 =$ _____

7 Complete:

$20 \div 10 =$ _____

8 How **many groups** of:

10 chickens in 96? ___ r ___

9 Write a **word problem** to match this number sentence:
$36 \div 6 = 6$

_____

_____

1 The **number** shown by the Base ten blocks is: UNIT 1 Q1

A 63   B 74   C 37   D 73

2 The **number** shown by the linking blocks (Unifix) is: 1 Q2

A 65   B 55   C 35   D 56

3 **True or false?**   2 Q1
The value of the 2 in 72 is 2 units. _____

4 **True or false?**   3 Q2
There are 3 digits in the number 705. _____

5 Write the **numeral** for forty-six. _____   1 Q3 / 3 Q4

6 Write 73 in **words**. _____   1 Q4 / 3 Q3
_____

7 Order these numbers from **smallest to largest**:   4 Q2
46, 73, 36, 67 _____

8 Write the **next number** after 89. _____   2 Q4 / 4 Q4

9 Circle the **larger number** in the pair: 48 or 84   2 Q2 / 5 Q4

10 Write the **largest possible** number using all of the digits: 4, 3, 5 _____   5 Q1 / 5 Q2

11 The **next number** after seventy-three is _____.   2 Q4 / 4 Q4

12 Order the numbers from **largest** (4) to **smallest** (1):   4 Q3
Fifty-five   _____
Seventy-two   _____
Twenty-seven   _____
Forty-six   _____

1 The **next number** after 209 is: UNIT 6 Q1

A 210   B 208   C 201   D 2010

2 The **numeral** for 80 + 7 is: 7 Q2 / 8 Q2

A 78   B 87   C 807   D 780

3 **True or false?**   7 Q4 / 8 Q4 / 9 Q2
The value of the underlined digit in 5807 is 8 hundred. _____

4 **True or false?**   10 Q3
The smaller number in the pair 168 and 681 is 681. _____

5 Write the number **before** 629. _____   6 Q2

6 Start at 52 and **count forward** by 3 four times.   6 Q3
_____

7 **Expand** 327. _____   7 Q3 / 8 Q3 / 9 Q4

8 Use the **number expander** to expand 407:   7 Q1 / 9 Q1

H	T	U

9 Draw the number 320 on the **abacus**:   8 Q1

H	T	U

10 Write the **numeral** for 1000 + 200 + 8. _____   9 Q3

11 Write 4000 + 200 + 50 + 1 in **words** as one number.   9 Q3
_____

12 Write the **number before** seven hundred and twenty **in words**.   6 Q2
_____

Score = [ ] /12

Score = [ ] /12

REVIEW TESTS: Units 11–22

1 $4 + 5 =$
A 8   B 10   C 9   D 11
UNIT 11 Q3 / 12 Q1 / 14 Q4

2 The **missing number** in $6 + \square = 10$ is:
A 3   B 5   C 10   D 4
13 Q3

3 **True or false?**
For the diagram, 3 more blocks are needed to make 10. _____
13 Q2

4 **True or false?**
$30 + 30 = 70$ _____
15 Q2

5 The **total** of the tens frames is: ____ + ____ = _____
11 Q1 / 12 Q1

6 Build to the **nearest 10**: $23 + \square = 30$
15 Q3

7 Start at 3 and **count on** by 5.
3, _____, _____, _____
12 Q2 / 12 Q3

8 Write a **number sentence** for:
+1 +1 +1 +1 +1
9 ... 14 _____
12 Q4

9 **Count on by 10** from 27. _____
12 Q4

10 **Complete**:

+	11	12	13	14
10				

16 Q3

11 **Add** ten to eight. _____
16 Q2

12 Find the **double** of each number from the answer bank:
a. 10 _____   100
b. 50 _____   20
c. 20 _____   80
d. 40 _____   40
15 Q4

Score = /12

1 The **missing number** in $7 + 1 = 1 + \square$ is:
A 8   B 6   C 5   D 7
UNIT 17 Q1 / 17 Q2 / 17 Q4

2 $70 + 18 =$
A 78   B 88   C 98   D 108
18 Q2 / 18 Q4 / 19 Q2 / 20 Q3 / 21 Q1 / 22 Q1

3 **True or false?**
Eight plus eleven equals twenty. _____
18 Q3

4 **True or false?**
The total of 32 buttons and 25 buttons is 57 buttons. _____
20 Q4 / 22 Q2

5 **Complete**:   7 t + 3 u
                    + 2 t + 4 u
                    _____
20 Q2 / 21 Q2

6 Complete the **tens frames** to show the number sentence and answer: $27 + 12 =$ ____
19 Q1

7 **Complete**:

+	12	22	32	42
6				

19 Q3

8 Find the **missing number**: $20 + \square = 40$
19 Q4

9 **Complete**:

T	U
2	3
+ 1	4

21 Q3

10 Write the **number sentence** for:
+10 +10 +1 +1
32 ... 54 _____
22 Q3

11 Find the **missing digits**: $72 + 1\square = \square 2$
21 Q4

12 Find the **total** of:
five plus thirteen plus twenty-one _____
22 Q4

Score = /12

1 10 **takeaway** 3 =   UNIT 23 Q3
A 3   B 10   C 7   D 8

2 **Complete the pattern**:   25 Q2
$39 - 4 = 35$ $29 - 4 = 25$ $19 - 4 = $ _____
A 4   B 25   C 15   D 5

3 **True or false?**   27 Q2
$47 - 10 = 27$ _____

4 **True or false?**   26 Q4
The missing number in $16 - \square = 10$ is 6 ___

5 Write a **number sentence** for: 23 Q1

_____

6 Start at 30 and **count back** by 6.   24 Q2 24 Q3
30, _____

7 **Complete**: $10 - 7 = \square$ 26 Q3

8 **Complete** the table: 27 Q4

–	19	29	39	49
10				

9 Write a **number sentence** for: _____   23 Q2 24 Q4 27 Q3 28 Q3

10 Find the **difference** between seventy-two and ten. _____   23 Q3 27 Q2

11 Complete the **tens frames** to show: 25 Q2 26 Q1
$20 - 7 = 13$

12 Complete the **sets of subtraction number sentences**:   28 Q4
$17 - 13 = \square$ $17 - \square = \square$

1 The **missing number** in $20 - \square = 12$ is: UNIT 29 Q4
A 7   B 8   C 32   D 12

2 The **difference between** 68 and 36 is: 30 Q1 31 Q1 32 Q3
A 23   B 32   C 14   D 35

3 **True or false?**   33 Q3 33 Q4
$33 + 26 = 59$ can be used
to check $59 - 26 = 33$ _____

4 **True or false?**   29 Q1 29 Q3 32 Q1 32 Q4
$48 - 17 = 35$ _____

5 **Find**:   30 Q1 31 Q2
$$\begin{array}{r} 7\,t + 3\,u \\ -\ 4\,t + 1\,u \\ \hline \end{array}$$

6 **Complete**:   31 Q3
$$\begin{array}{c|c} T & U \\ 8 & 9 \\ -\ 3 & 6 \\ \hline \end{array}$$

7 If Cooper had 27 cupcakes and gave 23 away, **how many** did he have left? _____   30 Q3

8 **Complete**:   31 Q4
$$\begin{array}{r} 9\ \square \\ -\ 5\ 6 \\ \hline \square\ 1 \end{array}$$

9 **Complete**:   33 Q3
$$7\,4 \quad \boxed{}$$
$$-\,6\,1 \qquad +\,6\,1$$

10 Use the **jump strategy** to find: 29 Q2 32 Q2
$88 - 47 = 88 - \square - 7 = \square$

11 Write a **number sentence** for: _____   32 Q2

12 Find the **difference between** sixty-four and forty-one and write your answer in words.   32 Q1
_____

Score = /12

Score = /12

REVIEW TESTS: Units 34–46

Unit 34 **Multiplication as repeated addition** .... page 26
Unit 35 **Multiplication as groups** .... page 27
Unit 36 **Multiplication as arrays** .... page 27
Unit 37 **Multiplication facts × 2** .... page 28
Unit 38 **Multiplication facts × 3** .... page 28

UNIT

1 4 **groups of** 3 people = (35 Q3)

A 12 people B 7 people
C 9 people D 16 people

2 3 × 10 = (38 Q4)

A 13 B 3 C 30 D 9

3 **True or false?** (34 Q3, 34 Q4)

2 × 8 = 2 + 2 + 2 + 2 ________

4 **True or false?** (36 Q3)

6 rows of 4 = 24 ________

5 Write a **number sentence** for: (35 Q1, 35 Q2, 36 Q1, 37 Q2, 38 Q2)

____

6 **True or false?** (36 Q2, 37 Q3)

The diagram and number sentence are equal.

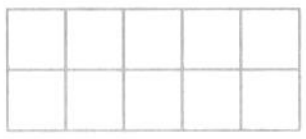

= 2 × 5 ________

7 Find the **missing digits**: (38 Q3)

3 groups of 10 = 2 groups of 10 + ☐ = ☐

8 Draw an **array** to show: 8 × 3 = (36 Q4, 37 Q4)

9 Complete the pictures to match the **number sentence**: (37 Q1)

7 groups of 2

= _____

10 Solve: seven **groups of** five = ____ (35 Q4)

11 **Expand**: (34 Q3, 34 Q4)

5 × 4 = ____ + ____ + ____ + ____ + ____

12 Circle the **larger** answer: (38 Q4)

3 × 5 or 2 × 7

Score = /12

Unit 39 **Multiplication facts × 4** .... page 29
Unit 40 **Multiplication facts × 5** .... page 29
Unit 41 **Multiplication facts × 6** .... page 30
Unit 42 **Multiplication facts × 7** .... page 30
Unit 43 **Multiplication facts × 8** .... page 31
Unit 44 **Multiplication facts × 9** .... page 31
Unit 45 **Multiplication facts × 10** .... page 32
Unit 46 **Mixed multiplication facts** .... page 32

UNIT

1 7 × 3 = (42 Q2, 44 Q2)

A 20 B 10 C 21 D 14

2 If 1 spider has 8 legs, then the **number of legs** on 9 spiders is: (41 Q1, 43 Q1)

A 72 legs B 17 legs
C 56 legs D 108 legs

3 **True or false?** (43 Q4, 45 Q3)

The product of 6 and 10 = 16 ________

4 **True or false?** (39 Q3)

9 × 6 = 6 × 9 ________

5 Write a **number sentence** for the array: (39 Q1, 39 Q2, 40 Q2, 41 Q3)

____

6 **Complete**: (40 Q4, 45 Q4)

×	3	6	8	1
5				

7 **Find**: (41 Q4, 42 Q4, 46 Q2)

$$\begin{array}{r} 6 \\ \times\ 7 \\ \hline \end{array}$$

8 Find the **missing numbers**: (39 Q4, 41 Q2, 46 Q3)

4 × ☐ = ☐ = 6 × 4

9 Write a **multiplication number sentence** for: (44 Q4)

15 ______________________

10 What are 4 **groups of** 7? (write the answer in words) ______________________ (42 Q3, 44 Q1)

11 Draw a **diagram** to show: 7 × 5 (40 Q3)

12 Movies cost $9 a show. **How many** times could Viv go if she has $54? ______ (44 Q1, 44 Q2, 44 Q3, 44 Q4)

Score = /12

REVIEW TESTS: Units 47–57

1 I can **take** 10 pens from 60 pens:
A 6 times   B 10 times
C 2 times   D 70 times
UNIT 48 Q2 / 48 Q3 / 50 Q1

2 20 **divided by** 2 =
A 4   B 20   C 2   D 10
49 Q4

3 **True or false?** _____
The diagram shows there are
4 groups of 3 stars in the picture:
52 Q1

4 **True or false?**
$10 \div 4 = 2 \text{ r } 2$ _____
52 Q4

5 **Share between** 5: ○○○○○
               ○○○○○
               ○○○○○
47 Q2 / 47 Q3

6 Draw a **number line** to show: $8 \div 2 =$
49 Q1

7 Draw an **array** to show: $14 \div 2 =$
49 Q3 / 50 Q4

8 **Complete**: $3 \times 15 = 5$ $15 \div 3 = \square$
50 Q3 / 51 Q1 / 51 Q2

9 **How many groups** of 2 children can be made from 21 children? _____
51 Q3

10 Write a **word question** that has the answer:
3 r 2 _____
52 Q3

11 A related division **number sentence** to
$5 \times 4 = 20$ is: _____
51 Q1 / 51 Q2

12 Draw a **diagram** to show how 4 boys shared 20 football cards evenly. 1 share = _____
47 Q4

1 492 rounded to the **nearest ten** is:
A 400   B 480   C 500   D 490
UNIT 53 Q1 / 54 Q1

2 The **missing number** of the space in the equation $7 + \square = 15$ is:
A 7   B 8   C 9   D 5
57 Q1

3 **True or false?** _____
$45 \div 9 = 5$ is a related division fact to the multiplication number sentence $9 \times 5 = 45$
56 Q3 / 56 Q4

4 **True or false?** _____
The missing number in $50 \div \square = 5$ is 5.
57 Q4

5 Round 414 to the **nearest hundred**. _____
53 Q2 / 54 Q2

6 Use the **jump strategy** to solve the addition equation: $46 + 23 =$ _____
55 Q1

7 Check the subtraction fact by **using addition**:
$36 - 16 = 20$ $20 +$ ____ = ____
56 Q2

8 Write the **missing number** in the space:
$5 \times \square = 20$
57 Q3

9 **True or false?** _____
1580 rounded to the nearest hundred is 1500.
53 Q4 / 54 Q3

10 Write a **number sentence** for the number line:
_____

55 Q2

11 Round each number to the **nearest hundred** and use these to estimate the answer:
$521 + 378 =$ _____
54 Q3 / 54 Q4

12 Draw a **number line** to show and find:
$20 \div 8 =$ ___ r ___
55 Q4

Score = /12   Score = /12

1 Use a calculator to find: 9 **groups of** 18 =   UNIT 59 Q3
A 27   B 126   C 162   D 621

2 Use a **calculator** to find: 87 − 69 =   58 Q2
A 18   B 22   C 31   D 156

3 **True or false?**   58 Q3
The difference between 95 and 78 is 17.
Use a calculator _____

4 **True or false?**   61 Q4
The missing numbers in the sequence
95, ☐, ☐, 80, 75, 70 are 90 and 85.

5 Complete the **number sequence**:   60 Q2
51, 53, 55, ____, ____, ____

6 Write a **number sentence** and solve: 58 Q4
Cody had 66 nails and 25 bolts. How many
items did he have altogether?

_____

7 Write the **number sequence** for the **rule**:   60 Q4
Start at 80 and count backwards by 3s to 71.

_____

8 Complete the **number sequence**:   61 Q2
120, 130, 140, ____, ____, ____

9 Write a **word problem** for: 42 × 8 = 336   59 Q1 / 59 Q4

_____

10 Write the **rule** for: 100, 95, 90, 85, 80   61 Q3

_____

11 Use a calculator to help find the **missing**   58 Q1
number: 78 + ☐ = 94

12 Complete the **number sequence** in **words**:   60 Q3
Fifty-one, fifty-three, fifty-five, _____,
_____, _____

---

1 A possible **number sentence** for: UNIT 64 Q1

⊗⊗   ⊗⊗   ⊗⊗   is
A 3 + 3   B 3 × 4   C 4 + 4   D 4 × 4

2 The **next number** in the sequence: 0, 8, 16, 24   62 Q1
is:
A 32   B 30   C 28   D 34

3 **True or false?** _____   64 Q3
The missing number in ☐ + 16 = 48 is 22

4 **True or false?** _____   63 Q1
To count forwards by 5 five times, starting at
20 we say: 20, 25, 30, 35, 40, 45

5 **Complete**:   62 Q4 / 63 Q2

+	10	20	30	40
11				

6 Complete the **number sequence**:   62 Q1
0, 3, 6, 9, 12, ____, ____, ____, ____

7 Write a **rule** for: 40, 37, 34, 31, 28   62 Q2 / 63 Q4

_____

8 Write a **number sentence** for: The **difference**   64 Q2
between 48 pencils and 25 pencils

_____

9 State the **tenth number** for the sequence: 62 Q3 / 63 Q3
6, 12, 18, 24 _____

10 Write a **word problem** for the number sentence   64 Q4
24 ÷ 4 = __ and solve it.

_____

11 Complete the **doubling sequence**:   62 Q1
3, 6, 12, ____, ____, ____

12 Write a **number sentence** and solve: 64 Q2
On the farm there are 10 cows, 12 sheep,
6 horses and 2 dogs. How many animals are
on the farm? _____

Score = ☐ /12   Score = ☐ /12

1 $\frac{1}{8}$ is ___ out of 8 **equal parts**. **UNIT 65 Q1**

A 2   B 1   C 8   D 4

2 The **fraction** of the group that is shaded is: **66 Q2**

A $\frac{1}{4}$ B $\frac{3}{2}$ C $\frac{3}{4}$ D $\frac{1}{2}$

3 True or false? **66 Q1**
$\frac{3}{8}$ of the rectangle has been shaded. _____

4 **True or false?** **65 Q4**
is $\frac{1}{2}$ shaded. _____

5 Complete: _____ out of _____ **65 Q3**
equal parts is shaded.

6 Shade **half** the group: **67 Q2**

7 Shade $\frac{3}{4}$ of the circle: **68 Q2**

8 **What fraction** of the group is shaded? **68 Q2**

9 Draw and colour $\frac{1}{2}$ a **rectangle**. **66 Q4 67 Q1 68 Q4**

10 Shade the **shape** to show $\frac{3}{4}$: **66 Q3**

11 Show 3 out of 4 **equal parts** of the group: **65 Q2 65 Q3**

12 Draw a picture of a tree and colour **half**. **67 Q3 67 Q4**

Score = ⬜ /12

1 As a **number**, five eighths is written: **UNIT 71 Q1**

A $\frac{1}{5}$ B $\frac{3}{8}$ C $\frac{8}{5}$ D $\frac{5}{8}$

2 $\frac{1}{4}$ **of a group** of 4 squares is: **69 Q3**

A   B
C   D

3 **True or false?** **70 Q1**
= $\frac{5}{10}$ _____

4 **True or false?** **71 Q2**
In words, $\frac{2}{4}$ = one quarter. _____

5 Shade $\frac{7}{10}$ of the **group**: **69 Q3 70 Q3**

6 What **part** of has been shaded? ____ **69 Q1**

7 Draw a **picture** to show three quarters. **71 Q4**

8 Place $\frac{8}{10}$ on the **number line**. **70 Q4**

0      $\frac{10}{10}$

9 Draw a circle and show $\frac{1}{4}$. **69 Q4**

10 Write $\frac{7}{10}$ in **words**. _____ **71 Q2**

11 Draw a **number line** and show $\frac{3}{10}$ on it. **70 Q4**

12 Write the fraction in **words** that describes: **69 Q1 70 Q2 71 Q2 71 Q3**

_____

Score = ⬜ /12

Excel Start Up Maths Year 2

☞ **Answers on page 99**

1 (coin) is **worth**:   `UNIT 72 Q1`

A $50   B 20c   C 5c   D 50c

2 10c + 10c + 10c + 10c + 10c =   `74 Q2`

A 50c   B 5c   C 10c   D $1

3 **True or false?**   `73 Q3`

Two (note) makes $100 _____

4 **True or false?** (note) is worth $5 _____   `73 Q1`

5 Order the set of coins from **smallest** to **largest**   `74 Q1`
value: 50c, 5c, 20c, $2 _____

6 Circle the coin of the **greatest value**:   `72 Q2`
50c, 5c, $2, 20c

7 Find the **total** of: `73 Q2`
$50 + $20 + $10 = _____

8 Match the price tag to the **total** of the money: `74 Q3`
$5 + $2 + 50c + 20c + 5c

$7.75 $7.25 $8.75

9 How much **more** would be needed to make   `73 Q4`
$50?

(note) + (note) + (note) + _____

10 **Draw** how many 20c coins are needed to make   `72 Q4`
$1.

11 Write the **total** of: $50, $2, $1, 50c, 5c _____   `72 Q3`
`74 Q4`

12 Write **3 different combinations** of money   `74 Q3`
that could be used to pay for this gift.

$6.45 _____
_____
_____

Score = ____ /12

---

1 15 **plus** 7 is: `UNIT 77 Q4`
A 20   B 13   C 22   D 23

2 The **missing number** in the pattern: `75 Q1`
22, ___, 30, 34, 38 is: `75 Q2`
A 24   B 26   C 28   D 18

3 **True or false?** _____   `77 Q1`
A number sentence for: `78 Q1`
is 11 + 3 = 14

4 **True or false?** _____   `75 Q3`
The pattern starting at 0 and counting
forwards by 3s is: 0, 3, 6, 9, 12, …

5 Complete the **pattern**:   `76 Q1`
△, ○, △, △, ○, △, ____, ____, ____

6 Write as a **number sentence** and solve: `77 Q2`
Four stars add nine stars _____

7 Write as a **word problem** and solve: 12 − 7 =   `77 Q3`
`78 Q3`
_____

8 Describe the **pattern** in words: `76 Q2`
○, △, ☆, ○, △, ☆ _____

9 Describe the **pattern** in words: `75 Q4`
60, 64, 68, 72, 76 _____

10 Write as a **number sentence** and solve: `78 Q2`
The **difference between** 19 and 9 cars.

_____

11 Solve and write the answer in **words**:   `78 Q4`
17 minus 11 = _____

12 Create your own **pattern** and write the rule.   `76 Q4`

_____
_____

Score = ____ /12

REVIEW TESTS: Units 79–90

1 [triangle shape] is called a | UNIT 79 Q1
- A circle   B square
- C rectangle   D triangle

2 A **square** has | 80 Q2 / 81 Q4 / 82 Q4
- A 4 corners   B 3 corners
- C 6 corners   D 8 corners

3 **True or false?** | 84 Q1
A [cube shape] has 6 faces. _____

4 **True or false?** | 80 Q4 / 81 Q3 / 82 Q2
Two squares have a total of 6 sides. _____

5 **Describe** the shape: [rectangle] | 79 Q4
_____

6 Circle the shape which is a **triangle**: | 80 Q3 / 81 Q1
[triangle]   [circle]   [square]

7 **Draw** a circle. | 79 Q1 / 81 Q2 / 82 Q1

8 Name the **shape** of the shaded face: [cylinder] | 83 Q1
_____

9 Name this **3D shape**: [cube] | 83 Q3
_____

10 How many **edges** does this 3D shape have? _____ [triangular prism] | 80 Q1 / 84 Q3

11 **Name** the shape: [parallelogram] | 82 Q1 / 82 Q3
_____

12 Draw a **cylinder**. | 83 Q3 / 84 Q4

1 The **longest** object is: | UNIT 85 Q1
- A pencil   B football field
- C car   D ruler

2 The **area** of [grid] is | 89 Q1
- A 4 squares   B 6 squares
- C 2 squares   D 8 squares

3 **True or false?** A curvy line could be measured with a piece of string. _____ | 86 Q4

4 **True or false?** The area of a table top could be measured with the palm of your hand. _____ | 88 Q3

5 Circle the object with the **largest area**: | 88 Q2
a pancake   a cupcake   a garbage bin lid

6 Order the pencils from **shortest** (1) to **longest** (3) [pencils] | 86 Q2

7 Estimate the **length** of the line in cm using your finger. _____ _____ | 85 Q3

8 Find the **area** of: [shape] _____ squares | 89 Q3

9 Order the areas from **smallest** (1) to **largest** (3) [grids] | 90 Q3 / 90 Q4

10 Circle the object with the **smaller** area: | 90 Q1 / 90 Q2
Pizza   slice of bread

11 Describe how you could measure the **area** of the floor of your classroom. _____ | 88 Q4

12 Draw an **area** of 12 squares. | 89 Q4

Score = [ ] /12   Score = [ ] /12

1 In the model [cube model] there are:

A 8 cubes   B 2 cubes
C 16 cubes   D 4 cubes

UNIT 92 Q1, 92 Q2, 92 Q3, 93 Q1

2 The **volume** of water in the container is:

A 1 L   B 2 L   C $\frac{1}{2}$ L   D 1$\frac{1}{2}$ L

93 Q3

3 **True or false?** The watermelon weighs more than the oranges. _____

94 Q1

4 **True or false?** A bird is heavier than an elephant. _____

95 Q1, 95 Q2

5 Circle the object with the **greater capacity**:

bucket   water tank

91 Q2

6 Circle the **larger model**:

93 Q2

7 Draw the number of apples to make the scales **balance**:

94 Q3

8 Complete the scales: 2 apples are **heavier** than 5 strawberries.

95 Q3

9 A container of milk could be **measured** with _____ (bucket, measuring jug, medicine cup.)

91 Q3

10 Give an object **heavier** than a brick. _____

95 Q2

11 If 1 apple = 10 grapes, make the scales **balance**:

95 Q4

12 Draw a model that has a **volume** of 12 cubes.

92 Q1, 93 Q1

Score = ____ /12

---

1 The **clock face** shows:

A a quarter past 12
B a quarter to 3
C 3 o'clock   D half past 6

UNIT 99 Q3

2 How many **minutes** are in 1 hour?

A 10   B 120   C 30   D 60

99 Q1

3 **True or false?** [clock] = half past 5

_____

97 Q2

4 **True or false?** [clock] is later than [clock]

_____

96 Q4

5 Write the **time** for: [clock]

_____

96 Q2

6 Draw a **quarter past** 6 on the watch face: [watch]

98 Q3

7 Add the times to the table to show the **earliest** (a) to the **latest** (c) times:

a quarter to 4   a quarter past 2   half past 6

a	b	c

97 Q4

8 Write the **time** shown: _____ [clock]

98 Q2

9 Complete the **hour hand** for the time, a quarter to 6: [clock]

99 Q2

10 Draw the hands to show the time is **half past 8**. [clock]

97 Q3

11 What time is one hour **later** than the clock face? _____ [clock]

97 Q1, 97 Q2

12 Draw a clock and show the time a **quarter to 2**.

99 Q4

Score = ____ /12

REVIEW TESTS: Units 100–112

1 5:15 written in **words** is: *UNIT 100 Q2 / 101 Q4*
A five thirty   B five fifteen
C six fifteen   D five o'clock

2 The **month** which is in **Summer** is: *103 Q2 / 103 Q3*
A May   B September
C December   D June

3 **True or false?** *101 Q1*
[3 : 45] is a quarter to 3. _____

4 **True or false?** *104 Q1*
There are 14 days in a fortnight. _____

5 Write the time seven thirty in **numbers**. _____ *100 Q2*

6 Write **quarter past 5** on the digital clock: [:] *101 Q1*

7 **Expand** the abbreviated month name. *102 Q4*
Nov _____

8 Circle the **coldest month** on this list: *103 Q4*
July   December   March

9 Which date is the **last Sunday** of the month? _____ *104 Q4*

January

S	M	T	W	Th	F	S
		1	2	3	4	5
6	7	8	9	10	11	12
13	14	15	16	17	18	19
20	21	22	23	24	25	26
27	28	29	30	31		

10 On which **day** of the week is the 16th January? (see Question 9) _____ *104 Q2*

11 List the names of the **months** in Autumn. *103 Q1 / 103 Q2 / 103 Q3 / 103 Q4*
_____

12 How much time has **passed** between: *100 Q1 / 100 Q2 / 100 Q3 / 100 Q4 / 104 Q1 / 104 Q2 / 104 Q3 / 104 Q4*
[8 : 30] and nine fifteen in the morning?
_____

1 The square has been **turned**: *UNIT 111 Q1*
A a $\frac{1}{4}$ turn to the left   B a $\frac{1}{4}$ turn to the right
C $\frac{1}{2}$ a turn to the right   D a whole turn

2 The **smallest angle** is: *112 Q1*
A   B   C   D

3 **True or false?** _____ *108 Q1 / 108 Q2 / 108 Q4*
[ ]→[ ] is a slide to the left.

4 **True or false?** _____ *112 Q2*
is called a right angle.

5 Describe the **position** of the letter L. _____ *105 Q2 / 105 Q4*

T	G	Z
C	F	V
W	Y	L

6 What is the letter in the **middle**? (in Question 5) ____ *105 Q1 / 105 Q3*

7 **Flip** the shape down: *109 Q1 / 109 Q2*

8 **Rotate** the triangle a **quarter turn** to the right: *110 Q1 / 110 Q2 / 110 Q3*

9 Draw an **angle** that is **smaller** than: *112 Q3 / 112 Q4*

10 Shade the **spinner** to show a **half turn** to the right: *111 Q3*

11 Give the **position** of ☺. _____ *107 Q1*

	A	B	C
3	≈	@	☆
2	○	%	☺
1	◇	▲	□

12 Give **directions** from ◇ to @. (see Question 11) _____ *106 Q3 / 106 Q4 / 107 Q2 / 107 Q3*

Score = [ ] /12

Score = [ ] /12

1 It is _____ that the sun will rise tomorrow. UNIT 113 Q1
  A **impossible**   B **unlikely**
  C **likely**   D **certain**

2 If a 6 sided die was rolled,   A 9   B 6   113 Q2
  it would be **impossible** to roll a: C 4   D 1

3 **True or false?** If a coin was tossed, a Head or   114 Q1
  Tail are the two possible results. _____

4 **True or false?**   114 Q1 / 114 Q2 / 114 Q3 / 114 Q4

  ⊢⊣⊣⊣ = 6 _____

5 What was the **most** popular   115 Q1 / 115 Q2
  colour on the graph?

  _____
  Red Green Blue

6 Look at the tick sheet.   116 Q2
  What was the **least**
  common number? _____

  1 | ✓✓✓
  2 | ✓✓✓✓
  3 | ✓✓✓✓✓✓
  4 | ✓✓✓

7 Create a **tally chart**   114 Q1 / 114 Q2 / 114 Q3
  from this information.

	Tally	Total
△		
○		
□		

  △ ○ □ □ □
  ○ △ △ △
  ○ ○ ○ △ △

8 Which area is the spinner **most**   113 Q3
  likely to land on? _____

9 What is the **most**   114 Q4
  popular pet? _____

  dog | ⊢⊣⊣⊣⊣ ⊢⊣⊣⊣⊣
  cat | ⊢⊣⊣⊣⊣ ||||
  bird | ||||

10 Draw a **graph** for the   115 Q3
  information in Question 9.

11 In this survey, **how many**   114 Q1 / 114 Q2 / 114 Q3 / 114 Q4
  people were questioned? _____

  1 | ⊢⊣⊣⊣⊣ ||
  2 | ⊢⊣⊣⊣⊣ |||
  3 | |||

12 Write **2 questions** about this graph: 116 Q1 / 116 Q2 / 116 Q3 / 116 Q4

  _____
  _____
  A   B   C

---

1 The **total** number of 15 frogs and 41 frogs is: UNIT 117 Q3
  A 40 frogs   B 26 frogs
  C 65 frogs   D 56 frogs

2 20 **shared between** 4 is: 120 Q1
  A 2   B 10   C 4   D 5

3 **True or false?** $\begin{array}{r} 9 \\ \times\ 6 \\ \hline 54 \end{array}$ _____   119 Q3

4 **True or false?** The number sentence that   118 Q1
  matches the number line is $69 - 45 = 24$

  -1 -1 -1 -1   -10   -10
  _____
  45   69

5 Find the   117 Q1
  total of: T U + T U   _____

6 Find the **difference** between 42 and 21. _____   118 Q2

7 **Complete**:   119 Q4

×	4	7	8	1
3				

8 **Find:** $50 \div 5 =$ _____   120 Q3

9 Find the **missing digits**:   118 Q4

  $\begin{array}{r} 9\ 7 \\ -\ \square\ 3 \\ \hline 2\ \square \end{array}$

10 Write the **number sentence** for: 119 Q1

  ◯◯ ◯◯ ◯◯ ◯◯ ◯◯   _____

11 If there are 5 chickens in each of 6 pens and   120 Q4
  one chicken left outside, **how many** chickens
  are there altogether?   ___ ÷ 6 = 5 r 1

12 If $\begin{array}{r} 7 \\ \times\ 5 \\ \hline 35 \end{array}$ then **complete** $35 \div 5 =$ ___   119 Q3 / 120 Q2
  and $35 \div 7 =$ ___

Score = _____ /12

Score = _____ /12

Unit 1 Page 10

1 a 27 b 39 c 56 d 83 2 a 42 b 91 c 78 d 16 3 a 19 b 65 c 37 d 50 4 a eleven b forty-eight c fifty-three d ninety-nine 5 6 6 28 7 73 8 fourteen 9 fifty-three

Unit 2 Page 10

1 a 2 tens b 2 units c 2 units d 2 units 2 a 91 b 53 c 40 d 98 3 a 47 b 79 c 24 d 66 4 a 50 b 77 c 82 d 31 5 2 units 6 75 7 11 8 20 9 58

Unit 3 Page 11

1 a 423 b 739 c 208 d 985 2 a 3 b 3 c 2 d 3 3 a eight hundred and fifty-two b nine hundred and seventeen c one hundred and five d four hundred 4 a 311 b 640 c 703 d 958 5 127 6 3 7 three hundred and ninety 8 876 9 386

Unit 4 Page 11

1 a 9 b 3 c 1 d 0 2 a 49, 53, 76, 85 b 114, 124, 134, 140 c 237, 475, 682, 856 d 105, 209, 403, 507 3 a 65, 57, 56, 6 b 520, 420, 321, 48 c 900, 883, 875, 861 d 310, 301, 130, 103 4 a 100 b 105 c 301 d 866 5 2 6 520, 529, 566, 580 7 918, 908, 890, 809 8 778 9 True

Unit 5 Page 12

1 a 234 b 789 c 104 d 357 2 a 876 b 953 c 754 d 980 3 a 57, 75, 89, 98 b 97, 101, 108, 115 c 527, 666, 785, 896 d 123, 231, 312, 321 4 a 96 b 170 c 351 d 111 5 136 6 321 7 426, 428, 604, 624 8 764 9 True

Unit 6 Page 12

1 a 207 b 786 c 397 d 429 2 a 728 b 855 c 406 d 289 3 a 38 b 42 c 46 d 55 4 a 44 b 40 c 38 d 29 5 911 6 335 7 44 8 46 9 13

Unit 7 Page 13

1 a [3 T 7 U] b [5 T 6 U] c [7 T 2 U] d [9 T 0 U] 2 a 26 b 43 c 91 d 79 3 a 10 + 7 b 60 + 6 c 80 + 4 d 90 + 7 4 a 6 tens b 9 units c 1 unit d 0 units 5 [1 T 7 U] 6 64 7 30 + 5 8 1 ten 9 e.g.

= 73

Unit 8 Page 13

1 a 352 b 444 c 821 d 602 2 a 625 b 971 c 439 d 806 3 a 100 + 50 + 7 b 700 + 8 c 500 + 50 + 5 d 200 + 20 4 a 3 b 1 c 5 d 3 5 721 6 363 7 800 + 10 + 1 8 0 9 753 = seven hundred and fifty-three

Unit 9 Page 14

1 a 8476 b 3791 c 2246 d 1195 2 a 1 unit b 8 hundreds c 7 thousands d 9 tens 3 a 6325 b 1400 c 7705 d 9851 4 a 6000 + 600 + 60 + 6 b 1000 + 500 + 7 c 9000 + 700 + 90 + 5 d 5000 + 900 + 1 5 6298 6 9 tens 7 2460 8 3000 + 300 + 50 9

Th H T U

Unit 10 Page 14

1 a 8763 b 9210 c 8544 d 7543 2 a 1238 b. 2479 c 1479 d 1348 3 a 79 b 147 c 2785 d 3840 4 a 30, 47, 58, 76 b 109, 156, 170, 185 c 1146, 1298, 1432, 1785 d 7046, 7736, 7856, 7896 5 8641 6 1367 7 4329 8 4782, 5893, 6115, 8908 9 876, 867, 786, 768, 678, 687

Unit 11 Page 15

1 a 5 + 4 = 9 b 3 + 2 = 5 c 7 + 5 = 12 d 8 + 4 = 12 2 a 6 + 5 = 11 b 9 + 4 = 13 c 7 + 6 = 13 d 5 + 8 = 13 3 a 6 b 8 c 8 d 5 4 a 9 b 8 c 12 d 15 5 6 + 3 = 9 6 3 + 10 = 13 7 9 8 12 9 7 + 3 + 4 = 14

Unit 12 Page 15

1 a 12 b 11 c 14 d 13 **2** a 18 b 22 c 23 d 21 **3** a 30 b 37 c 45 d 55 **4** a 12 e.g.

(number line: +1 +1 +1 +1, 8 9 10 11 12)

b 13 (number line: +1 +1 +1 +1 +1 +1 +1, 6 to 13)   c 15 (number line: +1 +1 +1 +1 +1 +1, 9 to 15)   d 12 (number line: +1 +1 +1 +1 +1 +1 +1, 5 to 12)

5 16 **6** 24 **7** 33 **8** 15   (number line: +1 +1 +1 +1 +1 +1 +1, 8 to 15)   **9** 23

Unit 13 Page 16

1 a 3 b 4 c 6 d 2 **2** a 8 + 2 = 10 b 5 + 5 = 10 c 1 + 9 = 10 d 3 + 7 = 10 **3** a 8 b 4 c 1 d 0 **4** a 4, 6; 12 b 8, 2; 14 c 9, 1; 15 d 3, 7; 15 **5** 5 **6** 9 + 1 = 10 **7** 6 **8** 6, 4; 15 **9** 60 40; 170

Unit 14 Page 16

1 a 8 + 8 = 16 b 1 + 1 = 2 c 4 + 4 = 8 d 6 + 6 = 12 **2** a 3 + 3 = 6 b 5 + 5 = 10 c 7 + 7 = 14 d 10 + 10 = 20 **3** a 4 + 4 = 8 b 6 + 6 = 12 c 5 + 5 = 10 d 7 + 7 = 14 **4** a 4 b 18 c 20 d 6 **5** 5 + 5 = 10 **6** 6 + 6 = 12 **7** 8 + 8 = 16 **8** 14 **9** a 24 b 30 c 40

Unit 15 Page 17

1 a 3, 30 b 5, 50 c 8, 80 d 9, 90 **2** a 20 b 60 c 80 d 40 **3** a 8 b 5 c 3 d 6 **4** a 40, 60; 120 b 80, 20; 110 c 70, 30; 140 d 50, 50; 120 **5** 9, 90 **6** 100 **7** 7 **8** 30, 70; 150 **9** 3 + 5 + 7 = 15 blocks

Unit 16 Page 17

1 a 3 + 10 = 13 b 7 + 10 = 17 c 6 + 10 = 16 d 1 + 10 = 11 **2** a 15 b 19 c 18 d 12 **3** a 26 b 29 c 31 d 45

4 a

+	1	2	3	4
10	11	12	13	14

b

+	7	8	9	10
10	17	18	19	20

c

+	5	6	7	8
10	15	16	17	18

d

+	11	12	13	14
10	21	22	23	24

5 4 + 10 = 14 **6** 16 **7** 22 **8**

+	25	26	27	28
10	35	36	37	38

9

+	19	7	26	32
10	29	17	36	42

Unit 17 Page 18

1 a 5, 5 b 8, 8 c 9, 9 d 9, 9 **2** a 2 b 6 c 3 d 5 **3** a 5 + 2 = 2 + 5 b 3 + 0 = 0 + 3 c 4 + 5 = 5 + 4 d 1 + 7 = 7 + 1 **4** a 2, 6 b 1, 5 c 7, 2 d 4, 1 **5** 7, 7 **6** 6 **7** 5 + 2 **8** 0, 9

9 They have the same answer.

6 + 2 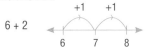   2 + 6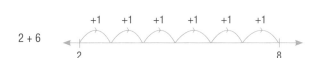

Unit 18 Page 18

1 a 10 + 6 = 16 b 7 + 5 = 12 c 3 + 12 = 15 d 15 + 4 = 19 **2** a 19 b 12 c 16 d 14 **3** a 6 + 2 = 8 b 9 + 4 = 13 c 7 + 12 = 19 d 4 + 13 = 17 **4** a 18 b 15 c 12 d 17 **5** 12 + 6 = 18 **6** 14 **7** 11 + 7 = 18 **8** 16 **9** 17

Unit 19 Page 19

1 a 20 + 17 = 37 b 14 + 15 = 29 c 12 + 14 = 26 d 12 + 21 = 33 **2** a 27 b 49 c 39 d 26

3 a

+	1	11	21	31
5	6	16	26	36

b

+	12	22	32	42
3	15	25	35	45

c

+	4	14	24	34
4	8	18	28	38

d

+	6	16	26	36
10	16	26	36	46

4 a 10 b 13 c 12 d 21 **5** 13 + 24 = 37 **6** 28 **7**

+	15	25	35	45
2	17	27	37	47

8 22 **9** 15 + 14 = 29, e.g.   (dots diagram) = 29

Unit 20 Page 19

1 a 44 + 12 = 56 b 22 + 52 = 74 c 32 + 26 = 58 d 20 + 43 = 63 **2** a 78 b 93 c 89 d 95 **3** a 75 b 49 c 98 d 58
4 a 38 pencils b 84 books c 79 buttons d 68 balls **5** 91 + 8 = 99 **6** 99 **7** 76 **8** 58 trees **9** e.g. 23 + 35 = 58
41 + 17 = 58

Unit 21 Page 20

1 a 45 b 69 c 89 d 93 **2** a 9 t + 7 u b 7 t + 9 u c 9 t + 6 u d 7 t + 6 u **3** a 51 b 69 c 89 d 78 **4** a 4, 8 b 8, 7 c 2, 3 d 4, 4
5 59 **6** 7 t + 7 u **7** 77 **8** 1, 4 **9** 14 + 12 + 1 = 27 people

Unit 22 Page 20

1 a 78 b 94 c 69 d 39 **2** a 68 hats b 57 scarves c 76 shoes d 82 gloves **3** a 72 b 81 c 74 d 76 **4** a 36 b 37 c 33 d 46
5 69 **6** 87 sunglasses **7** 73 **8** 46 **9** 83

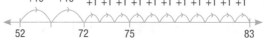

Unit 23 Page 21

1 a 7 – 2 = 5 b 12 – 5 = 7 c 9 – 4 = 5 d 11 – 7 = 4 **2** a 9 b 7 c 3 d 7 **3** a 6 b 3 c 3 d 2 **4** a 7 b 7 c 5 d 6 **5** 14 – 7 = 7
6 6 **7** 2 **8** 4 **9** 6, e.g.

Unit 24 Page 21

1 a 3 b 6 c 8 d 14 **2** a 27 b 23 c 20 d 18 **3** a 22 b 20 c 10 d 7 **4** a 5 e.g.

b 4 e.g.   c 7 e.g.   d 7 e.g.

5 11 **6** 15 **7** 16 **8** 8   **9** 18

Unit 25 Page 22

1 a 9 b 8 c 7 d 6 e 5 f 7 g 8 h 9 **2** a 15, 25 b 14, 4 c 3, 13, 23 d 3, 13, 23 **3** a 4, 2 b 4, 3 c 6, 2 d 3, 7 e 6, 3 **4** a 12, 2
b 14, 4 c 22, 12 d 22, 12, 2 **5** a 8 b 7 c 6 d 5 **6** 1, 11, 21 **7** 4, 6 **8** 26, 16, 6 **9** e.g. 10 – 6 = 4, 9 – 5 = 4, 8 – 4 = 4, 7 – 3 = 4

Unit 26 Page 22

1 a 3 b 1 c 7 d 5 **2** a 6 b 4 c 2 d 0 **3** a 9 b 4 c 2 d 5 **4** a 1 b 5 c 8 d 3 **5** 4 **6** 3 **7** 10 **8** 4
9

Unit 27 Page 23

1 a 33 – 10 = 23 b 46 – 10 = 36 c 51 – 10 = 41 d 25 – 10 = 15 **2** a 11 b 36 c 25 d 47
3 a 52 e.g.   b 16, e.g.   c 35, e.g.

d 33, e.g.

4 a

–	21	31	41	51
10	11	21	31	41

b

–	18	28	38	48
10	8	18	28	38

c

–	47	57	67	77
10	37	47	57	67

d

–	63	73	83	93
10	53	63	73	83

5 68 – 10 = 58 **6** 38 – 10 = 28 **7** 27 e.g. **8**

–	59	69	79	89
10	49	59	69	79

9 52 – 20 = 32   52 – 32 = 20

Unit 28 Page 23

1 a 5 b 11 c 6 d 11 **2** a 8 b 10 c 7 d 6 **3** a 6 b 11 c 3 d 5 **4** a 8, 5 b 5, 6 c 2, 15 d 9, 6 **5** 5 **6** 7 **7** 4 **8** 5, 7 **9** 15, 15, 15

Unit 29 Page 24

1 a 27 b 21 c 36 d 6 **2** a 18 b 25 c 20, 14 d 10, 11 **3** a 32 b 23 c 23 d 17 **4** a 9 b 16 c 22 d 11 **5** 23 **6** 10, 24 **7** 22 **8** 12 **9** 21

Unit 30 Page 24

1 a 31 b 25 c 34 d 32 **2** a 43 b 34 c 53 d 51 **3** a 22 birds b 25 flowers c 25 books d 12 chocolates **4** a 12 b 31 c 22 d 55 **5** 23 **6** 42 **7** 32 apples **8** 34 **9** 47 − 5 = 42 so his answer is incorrect, 42 lollipops

Unit 31 Page 25

1 a 15 b 21 c 44 d 17 **2** a 2t + 2u b 5t + 2u c 4t + 4u d 2t + 2u **3** a 55 b 41 c 13 d 22 **4** a 3, 1 b 5, 6 c 8, 8 d 8, 7 **5** 42 **6** 3t + 5u **7** 12 **8** 6, 6 **9** 98 − 42 = 56   56 − 33 = 23

Unit 32 Page 25

1 a 43 b 44 c 21 d 5 **2** a 5, 14 b 30, 13 c 40, 31 d 6, 60 **3** a 59 − 27 = 32 b 83 − 51 = 32 c 98 − 27 = 71 d 88 − 46 = 42 **4** a 55 b 53 c 44 d 12 **5** 61 **6** 40, 41 **7** 78 − 27 = 51 **8** 4 **9** a 38 b 25

Unit 33 Page 26

1 a 14, 5 b 11, 5 c 12, 8 d 7, 6 **2** a 11, 11 b 26, 26 c 45, 45 d 43, 43 **3** a 14, 14, 46 b 22, 22, 39 c 32, 32, 58 d 62, 62, 85 **4** a 33 b 23 c 43 d 15 **5** 13, 6 **6** 33, 33 **7** 42, 42, 74 **8** 55 **9** No.

$$\begin{array}{r} 3\,6 \\ +\ 5\,3 \\ \hline 8\,9 \end{array}$$

answer 98 − 36 = 62 not 53

Unit 34 Page 26

1 a 35 b 27 c 15 d 60 **2** a 12, 12 b 40, 40 c 36, 36 d 16, 16 **3** a 7 + 7 = 14 b 6 + 6 + 6 + 6 + 6 = 30 c 10 + 10 + 10 + 10 = 40 d 9 + 9 + 9 = 27 **4** a False b True c True d False **5** 36 **6** 28 **7** 4 + 4 + 4 + 4 + 4 = 20 **8** False **9** 3 + 3 + 3 + 3 = 12, 4 + 4 + 4 = 12, 6 + 6 = 12, 2 + 2 + 2 + 2 + 2 + 2 = 12, 1 + 1 + 1 + 1 + 1 + 1 + 1 + 1 + 1 + 1 + 1 + 1 = 12

Unit 35 Page 27

1 a 24 b 6 c 15 d 18 **2** a 4, 16 b 4, 3, 12 c 5, 5, 25 d 3, 6, 18 **3** a 4 × 2 = 8 fish b 3 × 6 = 18 cats c 5 × 10 = 50 pencils d 2 × 5 = 10 cards **4** a 15 b 7 c 60 d 16 **5** 14 **6** 8, 2, 16 **7** 6 × 2 = 12 chickens **8** 30

9
```
OO OO OO OO
 O   O   O   O    = 36 children
OO OO OO OO
 O   O   O   O
OO OO OO OO
 O   O   O   O
```

Unit 36 Page 27

1 a 9 b 24 c 10 d 21 **2** a 3 rows of 5 = 15 b 4 rows of 6 = 24 c 3 rows of 8 = 24 d 2 rows of 10 = 20 **3** a 24 b 12 c 9 d 40
4 a ▢ = 6 b ▢ = 12 c ▢ = 6 d ▢ = 15 **5** 32 **6** 2 rows of 7 = 14

7 14 **8** ▢ = 9 **9** 6 × 1, 1 × 6, 3 × 2, 2 × 3

Unit 37 Page 28

1 a 6 b 14 c 2, 20 d 2, 4 2 a 20 b 12 c 10 d 14 3 a 2 × 4 = 8 b 2 × 8 = 16 c 2 × 2 = 4 d 2 × 9 = 18

4 a [ ] = 6 b [ ] = 20 c [ ] = 8 d [ ] = 2 5 2, 12 6 16 7 1 × 2 = 2

8 [ ] = 4 9

×	2	4	7	10
	2	4	8	14	20

Unit 38 Page 28

1 a 3 b 6 c 15 d 30 2 a 3 × 3 = 9 b 3 × 5 = 15 c 7 × 3 = 21 d 2 × 3 = 6 3 a 6 b 15 c 30 d 21 4 a 3 b 9 c 30 d 21 5 18

6 4 × 3 = 12 7 27 8 15

9

Unit 39 Page 29

1 a 4, 20 b 4, 32 c 2, 4, 8 d 6, 4, 24 2 a 12 b 28 c 40 d 16 3 a 8 b 28 c 36 d 4 4 a 12 b 10 c 5 d 32 5 7, 4, 28 6 20

7 40 8 1

9

1	2	3	4	5	6	7	8	9	10
11	12	13	14	15	16	17	18	19	20
21	22	23	24	25	26	27	28	29	30
31	32	33	34	35	36	37	38	39	40
41	42	43	44	45	46	47	48	49	50
51	52	53	54	55	56	57	58	59	60
61	62	63	64	65	66	67	68	69	70
71	72	73	74	75	76	77	78	79	80
81	82	83	84	85	86	87	88	89	90
91	92	93	94	95	96	97	98	99	100

c Every second number is a table from 2 and 4

Unit 40 Page 29

1 a 5 b 35 c 15 d 25 2 a 45 b 20 c 40 d 10 3 a [ ] = 5 b [ ] = 30 c [ ] = 10

d [ ] = 15 4 a

×	1	2	3	4
	5	5	10	15	20

b

×	5	6	7	8
	5	25	30	35	40

c

×	7	8	9	10
	5	35	40	45	50

d

×	1	3	5	7
	5	5	15	25	35

5 30 6 25 7 [ ] = 20 8

×	2	4	6	8
	5	10	20	30	40

9 5 × $5 = $25

Unit 41 Page 30

1 a 30 legs b 48 legs c 60 legs d 18 legs **2** a 6 b 60, 10 c 48, 8 d 12, 6 **3** a 24 b 36 c 54 d 42 **4** a 12 b 42 c 24 d 54
5 24 legs **6** 42, 7 **7** 30 **8** 60
9

Unit 42 Page 30

1 a 35 days b 49 days c 21 days d 70 days **2** a 49 b 35 c 21 d 7 **3** a 14 b 28 c 63 d 42 **4** a 70 b 63 c 14 d 49
5 42 days **6** 56 **7** 21 **8** 28
9

Unit 43 Page 31

1 a 80 legs b 48 legs c 32 legs d 24 legs **2** a 40 b 56 c 64 d 72 **3** a 8 b 8 c 8 d 8 **4** a 16 b 72 c 48 d 40 **5** 56 legs
6 24 **7** 8 **8** 32 **9** 24

Unit 44 Page 31

1 a 72 b 36 c 81 d 27 **2** a 63 b 54 c 9 d 90 **3** a 1, 9 b 2, 18 c 3, 27 d 4, 36 **4** a 7 × 9 b 9 × 9 c 3 × 9 d 6 × 9 **5** 45
6 36 **7** 5, 45 **8** 5 × 9 **9** 1 + 8 = 9, 2 + 7 = 9, 3 + 6 = 9; They all equal 9

Unit 45 Page 32

1 a 50 b 70 c 80 d 100 **2** a 10 b 1 c 4 d 90 **3** a 70 b 20 c 50 d 80 **4** a

×	1	2	3	4
10	10	20	30	40

b

×	5	6	7	8
10	50	60	70	80

c

×	7	8	9	10
10	70	80	90	100

d

×	9	7	5	3
10	90	70	50	30

5 40 **6** 7 **7** 60

8

×	8	6	4	2
10	80	60	40	20

9 70 pencils

Unit 46 Page 32

1 a 24 b 56 c 15 d 9 **2** a 18 b 20 c 30 d 64 **3** a 20, 10 b 18, 9 c 40 d 3, 9 **4** a ⬚⬚⬚⬚⬚⬚⬚ = 7
b ⬚ = 21 c ⬚ = 18 d ⬚ = 32 **5** 100 **6** 35 **7** 4, 12

8 20 ⬚

9

×	2	4	5	6
3	6	12	15	18
6	12	24	30	36
9	18	36	45	54

ANSWERS: Units 47–54

Unit 47 Page 33

1. a 3 b 3 c 3 d 2 for example:

2. a 5 b 2 c 3 d 6 3. a 7 b 3 c 2 d 5

4. a 5 apples b 5 biscuits c 5 stickers d 2 tennis balls 5. 2 6. 4 7. 3 8. 2 cupcakes

9.

20 ÷ 4 = 5

Unit 48 Page 33

1. a 4 b 3 c 5 d 6 2. a 8 b 4 c 2 d 1 3. a 9 b 10 c 6 d 2 4. a 5 b 6 c 10 d 6 5. 2 6. 5 7. 10 8. 6

9. e.g. 35 − 5 − 5 − 5 − 5 − 5 − 5 − 5 = 0, 7 pencils per child

Unit 49 Page 34

1. a 2 b 4 c 8 d 10

2. a 6 b 3 c 4 d 5

3. e.g. a b c d 4. a 3 b 4 c 10 d 9 5. 9

6. 2 7. 8. 9 9. e.g. 12 ÷ 3 = 4, 12 ÷ 4 = 3, 12 ÷ 6 = 2, 12 ÷ 2 = 6, 12 ÷ 12 = 1, 12 ÷ 1 = 12

Unit 50 Page 34

1. a 3 b 4 c 5 d 1 2. a 10 b 6 c 7 d 2 3. a 3 b 8 c 9 d 5 4. a 3 e.g. b 2 c 4

d 7 5. 2 6. 1 7. 3 8. 1 9. various, e.g. 3 children share 30 toys. Each have 10.

Unit 51 Page 35

1. a 6, 4 b 8, 5 c 6, 9 d 3, 10 2. a 10, 7 b 6, 3 c 8, 4 d 6, 5 3. a 7 groups b 5 groups c 5 groups d 4 groups

4. a 7 × 1 = 7, 1 × 7 = 7, 7 ÷1 = 7, 7 ÷ 7 = 1 b 5 × 2 = 10, 2 × 5 =10, 10 ÷ 5 = 2, 10 ÷ 2 = 5
c 3 × 4 = 12, 4 × 3 = 12, 12 ÷ 3 = 4, 12 ÷ 4 = 3 d 4 × 5 = 20, 5 × 4 = 20, 20 ÷ 4 = 5, 20 ÷ 5 = 4 5. 7, 6 6. 9, 70 7. 11

8. 2 × 10 = 20, 10 × 2 = 20, 20 ÷ 2 = 10, 20 ÷ 10 = 2 9. various, e.g. 3 dogs 4 legs each makes 12 legs altogether.

Unit 52 Page 35

1. a 3, 1 b 3, 1 c 2, 2 d 1, 2 2. a 5 b 4 c 6, 2 d 3, 2 3. a 2r3 b 3r3 c 4r1 d 6r2 4. a 3r1 b 2r3 c 2r6 d 1r3 5. 3, 3 6. 2r6

7. 6r1 8. 3r3 9. 8 sets and 1 left over

Unit 53 Page 36

1. a 50 b 60 c 70 d 100 2. a 200 b 200 c 400 d 400 3. a 600 b 100 c 400 d 900 4. a True b True c False d False 5. 20

6. 800 7. 500 8. True 9. 1500 as 75 rounds up to the nearest hundred

Unit 54 Page 36

1. a 490 b 310 c 610 d 120 2. a 300 b 300 c 500 d 900 3. a 3600 b 4700 c 5200 d 9500 4. a 30 + 70 = 100 b 10 + 70 = 80
c 40 + 50 = 90 d 80 + 10 = 90 5. 900 6. 700 7. 1200 8. 70 + 60 = 130 9. 20 + 10 + 20 + 20 = 70 seeds approximately

ANSWERS: Units 55–62

Unit 55 Page 37

1 a e.g.

b 55 c 54 d 51 **2** a 37 b 27 c 26 d 25 **3** a 30 b 20 c 20 d 25 **4** a 5 b 6 c 3 d 4 **5** 81
6 31 **7** 35 **8** 5 **9** various

Unit 56 Page 37

1 a 8, 24 b 9, 53 c 8, 37 d 6, 17 **2** a 7, 19 b 14, 25 c 28, 37 d 12, 42 **3** e.g. a 5, 9 b 6, 10 c 3, 8 d 7, 4
4 a 8, 16 b 4, 24 c 8, 40 d 7, 56 **5** 19, 17 **6** 12, 47 **7** e.g. 5, 4 **8** 6, 36
9

A	16	6	2
B	4	10	7
C	9	5	13

Unit 57 Page 38

1 a 9 b 5 c 11 d 19 **2** a 4 b 5 c 9 d 7 **3** a 6 b 7 c 7 d 4 **4** a 5 b 2 c 4 d 10 **5** 17 **6** 15 **7** 9 **8** 4
9 a × b + c − d ×

Unit 58 Page 38

1 a 84 b 84 c 151 d 117 **2** a 19 b 2 c 32 d 13 **3** a 128 b 69 c 8 d 124 **4** a 60 − 21 − 39 sweets b 97 + 56 = 153 items
c 79 + 56 = 135 pieces of lego d 96 − 76 = 20 stickers **5** 140 **6** 83 **7** 14 **8** 61 + 50 = 111 items **9** 35

Unit 59 Page 39

1 a 119 b 135 c 54 d 96 **2** a 25 b 36 c 59 d 48 **3** a 198 b 15 c 294 d 45 **4** a 25 × 6 = 150 doughnuts
b 180 ÷ 5 = 36 pencils c 135 ÷ 9 = 15 books d 32 × 9 = 288 toys **5** 216 **6** 16 **7** 200 **8** 8 × 26 = 208 Year 1s **9** various

Unit 60 Page 39

1 a 8, 10, 12 b 16, 18, 20 c 14, 12, 10 d 44, 42, 40 **2** a 12, 15, 18 b 30, 33, 36 c 21, 18, 15 d 51, 48, 45
3 a counting forwards by 2s b counting backwards by 3s c counting forwards by 2s d counting forwards by 3s
4 a 40, 42, 44, 46, 48, 50 b 50, 48, 46, 44, 42, 40 c 90, 87, 84, 81, 78, 75, 72 d 70, 73, 76, 79, 82, 85, 88 **5** 29, 31, 33
6 19, 22, 25 **7** counting by 3s **8** 3, 5, 7, 9, 11 **9** various

Unit 61 Page 40

1 a 20, 25, 30 b 65, 70, 75 c 35, 30, 25 d 85, 80, 75 **2** a 40, 50, 60 b 110, 120, 130 c 70, 60, 50 d 170, 160, 150
3 a 85, 90, 95, 100 b 110, 120, 130, 140 c 100, 95, 90, 85, 80 d 500, 490, 480, 470 **4** a 90, 95 b 70, 50 c 95, 85 d 200, 180
5 165, 170, 175 **6** 100, 90, 80 **7** 105, 110, 115, 120, 125 **8** 220, 240 **9** a 97, 102, 107 b 73, 63, 53 c 56, 61, 66

Unit 62 Page 40

1 a 16, 20, 24 b 28, 35, 42 c 36, 45, 54 d 24, 30, 36 **2** a start at 3 count forwards by 3 b start at 40 count forwards by 8
c start at 30 and count forwards by 6 d start at 20 and count forwards by 10 **3** a 20 b 30 c 50 d 100
4 a

+	10	20	30	40
4	14	24	34	44

b

+	30	40	50	60
6	36	46	56	66

c

+	4	14	24	34
6	10	20	30	40

d

+	6	16	26	36
3	9	19	29	39

5 32, 40, 48 **6** start at 50 and count forwards by 5 **7** 40 **8**

+	14	24	34	44
5	19	29	39	49

9 a 24, 34 b start at 19 and count forward by 5

Answers

89

Unit 63 Page 41

1 a 50, 55, 60, 65, 70, 75 b 50, 57, 64, 71, 78, 85 c 50, 47, 44, 41, 38, 35 d 50, 46, 42, 38, 34, 30

2 a

+	4	14	24	34
10	14	24	34	44

b

+	5	15	25	35
11	16	26	36	46

c

+	2	12	22	32
12	14	24	34	44

d

+	10	20	30	40
20	30	40	50	60

3 a 2 b 55 c 40 d 42 4 a start at 3 and count forwards by 3
b start at 40 and count forwards by 2 c start at 100 and count forwards by 100
d start at 1 and count forwards 2

5 50, 53, 56, 59, 62, 65 6

+	3	13	23	33
3	6	16	26	36

7 82 8 start at 20 and count forwards by 3 9 16, 32, 64

Unit 64 Page 41

1 a 8 + 5 = 13 b 9 − 3 = 6 c 3 × 5 = 15 d 12 ÷ 4 = 3 2 a 35 + 22 = 57 cats b 46 − 31 = 15 students c 5 × 7 = 35 balls
d 50 ÷ 5 = 10 groups 3 a 15 b 13 c 5 d 4 4 a 25 b 11 c 21 d 5 5 15 − 6 = 9 6 15 + 11 = 26 birds 7 6
8 various, 6 9 8 + 2 + 8 + 12 = 30 pets

Unit 65 Page 42

1 a 1 b 1 c 3 d 1 2 a 2 b 8 c 4 d 8 3 a 1, 2 b 1, 4 c 2, 4 d 3, 8 4 a 4 b 3 c 1 d 7 5 5 6 4 7 1, 4 8 1
9 e.g.

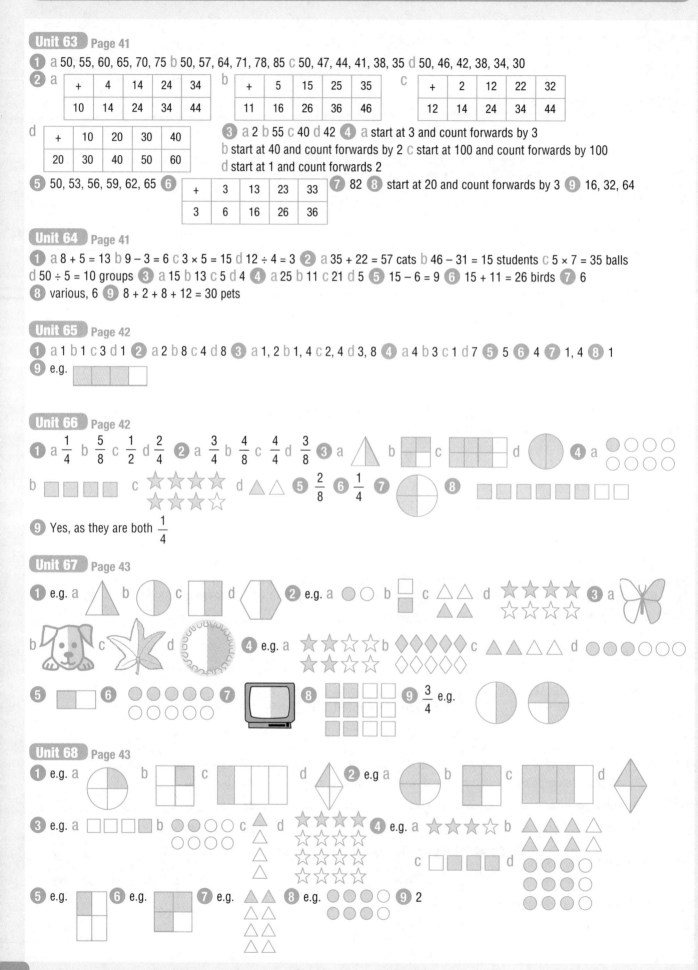

Unit 66 Page 42

1 a $\frac{1}{4}$ b $\frac{5}{8}$ c $\frac{1}{2}$ d $\frac{2}{4}$ 2 a $\frac{3}{4}$ b $\frac{4}{8}$ c $\frac{4}{4}$ d $\frac{3}{8}$ 3 a b c d 4 a
b c d 5 $\frac{2}{8}$ 6 $\frac{1}{4}$ 7 8

9 Yes, as they are both $\frac{1}{4}$

Unit 67 Page 43

1 e.g. a b c d 2 e.g. a b c d 3 a
b c d 4 e.g. a b c d

5 6 7 8 9 $\frac{3}{4}$ e.g.

Unit 68 Page 43

1 e.g. a b c d 2 e.g a b c d

3 e.g. a b c d 4 e.g. a b
c d

5 e.g. 6 e.g. 7 e.g. 8 e.g. 9 2

ANSWERS: Units 69–75

Unit 69 Page 44

1 a $\frac{3}{8}$ b $\frac{7}{8}$ c $\frac{4}{8}$ d $\frac{5}{8}$ 2 e.g. a 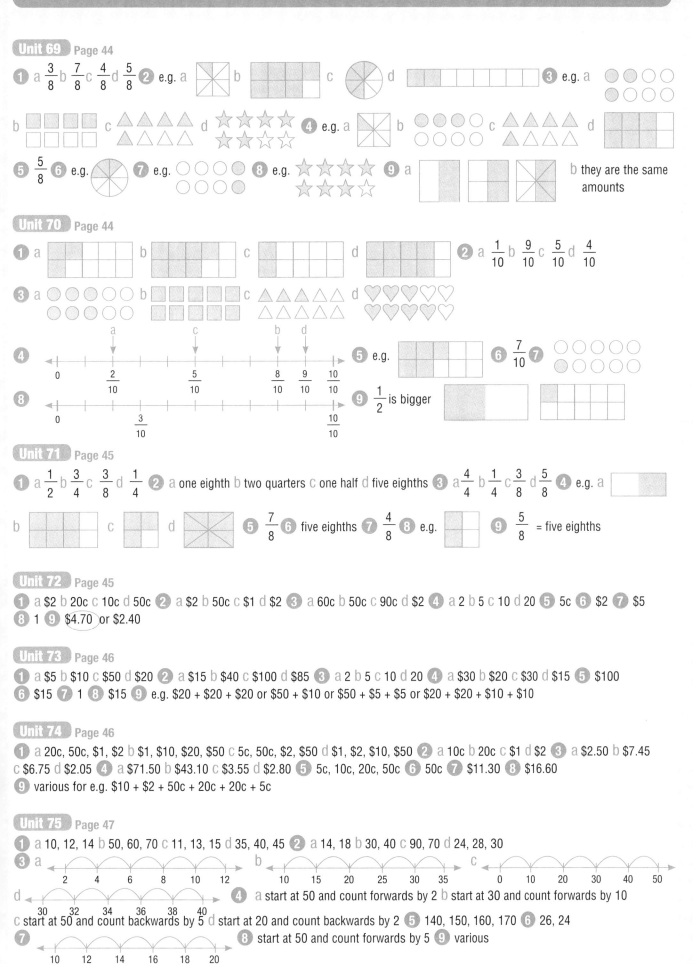 b c d 3 e.g. a

b c d 4 e.g. a b c d

5 $\frac{5}{8}$ 6 e.g. 7 e.g. 8 e.g. 9 a b they are the same amounts

Unit 70 Page 44

1 a b c d 2 a $\frac{1}{10}$ b $\frac{9}{10}$ c $\frac{5}{10}$ d $\frac{4}{10}$

3 a b c d

4 5 e.g. 6 $\frac{7}{10}$ 7

8 9 $\frac{1}{2}$ is bigger

Unit 71 Page 45

1 a $\frac{1}{2}$ b $\frac{3}{4}$ c $\frac{3}{8}$ d $\frac{1}{4}$ 2 a one eighth b two quarters c one half d five eighths 3 a $\frac{4}{4}$ b $\frac{1}{4}$ c $\frac{3}{8}$ d $\frac{5}{8}$ 4 e.g. a

b c d 5 $\frac{7}{8}$ 6 five eighths 7 $\frac{4}{8}$ 8 e.g. 9 $\frac{5}{8}$ = five eighths

Unit 72 Page 45

1 a $2 b 20c c 10c d 50c 2 a $2 b 50c c $1 d $2 3 a 60c b 50c c 90c d $2 4 a 2 b 5 c 10 d 20 5 5c 6 $2 7 $5
8 1 9 $4.70 or $2.40

Unit 73 Page 46

1 a $5 b $10 c $50 d $20 2 a $15 b $40 c $100 d $85 3 a 2 b 5 c 10 d 20 4 a $30 b $20 c $30 d $15 5 $100
6 $15 7 1 8 $15 9 e.g. $20 + $20 + $20 or $50 + $10 or $50 + $5 + $5 or $20 + $20 + $10 + $10

Unit 74 Page 46

1 a 20c, 50c, $1, $2 b $1, $10, $20, $50 c 5c, 50c, $2, $50 d $1, $2, $10, $50 2 a 10c b 20c c $1 d $2 3 a $2.50 b $7.45
c $6.75 d $2.05 4 a $71.50 b $43.10 c $3.55 d $2.80 5 5c, 10c, 20c, 50c 6 50c 7 $11.30 8 $16.60
9 various for e.g. $10 + $2 + 50c + 20c + 20c + 5c

Unit 75 Page 47

1 a 10, 12, 14 b 50, 60, 70 c 11, 13, 15 d 35, 40, 45 2 a 14, 18 b 30, 40 c 90, 70 d 24, 28, 30
3 a b c
d 4 a start at 50 and count forwards by 2 b start at 30 and count forwards by 10
c start at 50 and count backwards by 5 d start at 20 and count backwards by 2 5 140, 150, 160, 170 6 26, 24
7 8 start at 50 and count forwards by 5 9 various

Unit 76 Page 47

1 a □, △, ○ b ○, ☆, ☆ c ○, ○, □ d ☆, □, △ 2 a triangle, circle, circle b square, triangle, circle c circle, circle, square, circle, circle, triangle, circle, circle, star d square, square, square, circle, circle, circle, star, star, star
3 a ☆, ○, ☆, ☆, ○, ☆ b ○, ○, □, ○, ○, □ c □, ○, □ □, ○, □, □, ○, □ d ○, ○, ☆, ○, ○, ☆, ○, ○, ☆ 4 a – d various 5 ☆, ☆, ○ 6 star, star, circle repeated twice
7 ○, □, △, ○, □, △, ○, □, △ 8 various 9 a ⠂ ⠒ ⠿ b add one dot each time

Unit 77 Page 48

1 a 6 + 8 = 14 flies b 3 + 9 = 12 lady bugs c 12 + 4 = 16 butterflies d 10 + 2 = 12 spiders 2 a 4 + 5 = 9 biscuits b 7 + 9 = 16 cakes c 11 + 7 = 18 sandwiches d 13 + 6 = 19 burgers 3 various e.g. a 15 b 19 c 15 d 11 4 a 15 b 19 c 18 d 23
5 5 + 15 = 20 bugs 6 6 + 3 = 9 apples 7 various e.g. 10 8 14 9 subtract

Unit 78 Page 48

1 a 12 − 6 = 6 fish b 11 − 3 = 8 sharks c 13 − 7 = 6 starfish d 9 − 3 = 6 shells 2 a 7 − 2 = 5 footballs b 11 − 8 = 3 tennis balls c 10 − 9 = 1 golf ball d 12 − 5 = 7 netballs 3 various e.g. a 2 b 0 c 7 d 2 4 a 9 b 6 c 14 d 8 5 10 − 1 = 9 dolphins
6 3 cricket balls 7 various = 8 8 3 9 16 − 11

Unit 79 Page 49

1 a rectangle b triangle c square d circle 2 e.g. a ○ b ◺ c □ d ▭ 3 a yes b yes c no d yes
4 e.g. a pushed over rectangle with 4 straight sides b round shape, no straight lines c 3 straight sides d 4 straight sides, 2 longer
5 triangle 6 e.g. □ 7 yes 8 shaped like a diamond, with 4 straight sides 9 e.g. ⬡

Unit 80 Page 49

1 a 3 b 4 c 4 d 1 2 a 3 b 4 c 4 d 0 3 a yes b yes c yes d no 4 a c, d, e b a, e, f c f d a, b 5 4 6 4 7 no 8 A
9 various

Unit 81 Page 50

1 a no b yes c no d no 2 e.g. a □ b ▭ c △ d ○ 3 a 8 b 12 c 8 d 12 4 a 8 b 12 c 8 d 12
5 □ 6 △ △ 7 20 8 16 9 a. 4 b. none c. 4 d. 4

Unit 82 Page 50

1 e.g. a □ b ◇ c ▱ d ○ 2 a 1 b 4 c 4 d 4 3 a yes b no c no d yes 4 a 4 b 4 c 0 d 4
5 ▭ 6 4 7 No, yes, no 8 4 9 various

Unit 83 Page 51

1 a triangle b square c circle d rectangle 2 a 3 b 1 c 6 d 1 3 order d, c, b, a 4 a 6 b 3 c 2 d 6 5 triangle 6 3
7 order b, c, a 8 4 9 cylinder

Unit 84 Page 51

1 a 6 b 6 c 5 d 4 2 a 8 b 8 c 4 d 0 3 a 12 b 2 c 12 d 9 4 a ○ b □ c ▭ d ◇ 5 3 6 6
7 12 8 ○ 9 various

Unit 85 Page 52

1 a the snake 2 c the eraser 3 various (real lengths) a 2 cm b 3 cm c 5 cm d 8 cm 4 a string b ruler c finger d handspan
5 crocodile 6 first child 7 various (real length) 10 cm 8 ruler 9 crab, fish, crocodile, whale

Unit 86 Page 52

1 b the pea **2** c **3** various **4** a string b ruler c hand span d finger or ruler **5** book **6** No 2 **7** various **8** string
9 various (real lengths)

5cm

3cm   3cm

5cm

Unit 87 Page 53

1 2, 3, 4, 1 **2** 2, 3, 1, 4 **3** 1, 2, 3, 4 **4** 1, 3, 4, 2 **5** 2, 1 **6** 1, 2 **7** 1, 2 **8** 1, 2 **9** various

Unit 88 Page 53

1 a the book **2** d the basketball court **3** various **4** a stone b palm of hand c newspaper sheets d counter or palm of hand
5 doughnut **6** painting **7** various **8** newspaper sheets **9** middle one, as it takes up the most space

Unit 89 Page 54

1 a 4 squares b 3 squares c 6 squares d 4 squares **2** a 9 squares b 6 squares c 2 squares d 12 squares **3** a 9 squares
b 4 squares c 4 squares d 10 squares **4** various **5** 12 squares **6** 6 squares **7** 8 squares **8** various
9 various but larger than 5 squares

Unit 90 Page 54

1 4, 2, 3, 1 **2** 2, 1, 3, 4 **3** 3, 4, 2, 1 **4** 2, 1, 3, 4 **5** 1, 2 **6** 1, 2 **7** 1, 2 **8** 1, 2 **9** various

Unit 91 Page 55

1 1, 3, 2, 4 **2** a pool b milk container c water tank d water tank **3** a A b C c B d B **4** a B b C c 5 cups d A **5** 1, 2
6 bucket **7** C **8** 3 cups **9** various e.g. using a bucket

Unit 92 Page 55

1 a 4 b 4 c 4 d 4 **2** a 8 b 18 c 10 d 27 **3** 1, 3, 2, 4 **4** a 1st one b 1st one c 2nd one d 1st one **5** 8 **6** 36 **7** 3, 1, 2
8 2nd one **9** various (two unshaded)

Unit 93 Page 56

1 a 8 cubes b 8 cubes c 12 cubes d 4 cubes **2** 2, 2, 3, 1 **3** a 1 L b 500 mL c 1.5 L d 2 L **4** 3, 2, 4, 1 **5** 24 cubes
6 1st one **7** 750 mL **8** 1st one **9** 50 + 30 = 80 L

Unit 94 Page 56

1 a more b less c more d less **2** a brick b television c pile of books d bag of apples **3** a 3 apples b 4 apples c 2 apples
d 5 apples **4** a watermelon b strawberries c orange and pear d bananas **5** less **6** potato **7** 4 apples **8** apples
9 1 watermelon; potatoes are easier to pick up.

Unit 95 Page 57

1 2, 3, 1, 4 **2** 1, 2, 4, 3 **3** a

cat
elephant

b apple   orange

c

snake
dog

d

mouse
cat

4 a 5 strawberries b 10 strawberries c 25 strawberries d 3 strawberries **5** 3, 1, 2 **6** 3, 2, 1

7 ant
spider

8 7 strawberries **9** various

Unit 96 Page 57

1 a b c d 　**2** a 2 o'clock b 8 o'clock c 12 o'clock d 5 o'clock

3 a b c d 　**4** 2, 1, 4, 3　**5**　**6** 7 o'clock　**7**

8 3, 1, 2　**9** 60 minutes

Unit 97 Page 58

1 a b c d 　**2** a half past 10 b half past 9 c half past 6 d half past 2

3 a b c d 　**4** 2, 4, 1, 3　**5**　**6** half past 3　**7**

8 3, 1, 2　**9** 30 minutes

Unit 98 Page 58

1 a b c d 　**2** a quarter past 11 b quarter past 5 c quarter past 8 d quarter past 12

3 a b c d 　**4** d, c, a, b　**5**　**6** quarter past 11　**7**

8 c, a, b　**9** 2 hours and 15 minutes

Unit 99 Page 59

1 a 60 minutes b 15 minutes c 30 minutes d 120 minutes　**2** a b c d

3 a quarter to 4 b quarter to 11 c quarter to 8 d quarter to 6

4 a b c d 　**5** 180 minutes　**6** 　**7** quarter to 5　**8**

9 60 minutes

Unit 100 Page 59

1 c, d, a, b　**2** a 6: 15 b 9: 30 c 4: 00 d 7:45　**3** a ten fifteen b two o'clock c twelve forty-five d five thirty　**4** a half, 8 b 6 c 3 d 2

5 6:45　**6** 7:15　**7** one thirty　**8** half, 10　**9** c, a, b

Unit 101 Page 60

1 a 2:45 b 6:30 c 9:00 d 10:15　**2** a 1 b 12 c 9 d half, 4　**3** c, d, a, b　**4** a quarter past 7 b 9 o'clock c half past 1 d 3 o'clock

5 4:15　**6** half, 7　**7** quarter to 2　**8** five o'clock　**9** various

Unit 102 Page 60

1 a, c **2** c **3** c **4** a January b October c September d December **5** August **6** May **7** September **8** November
9 a 12 b January, February, March, April, May, June, July, August, September, October, November, December

Unit 103 Page 61

1 b, c, d **2** b, d **3** a, d **4** a, d **5** Winter **6** October **7** August **8** June, July **9** The wet season lasts about six months in summer and spring. The dry season lasts about six months in autumn and winter.

Unit 104 Page 61

1 a 12 b 7 c 14 d 31 **2** a Thursday b Friday c Monday d Sunday **3** a Yes b No c No d Yes **4** a 7th July b 30th July c 8th July d 17th July **5** 31 **6** Wednesday **7** April, September **8** 12th July **9** September = 30 days, October = 31 days and November = 30 days

Unit 105 Page 62

1 a Kasey b Arthur c Sophie d Charlie **2** a in the middle b top shelf, left c top shelf, right d bottom shelf, right **3** a apple b milk c cup cake d roll **4** a top shelf, middle b bottom shelf, right c middle shelf, left d bottom shelf, middle **5** Alex **6** middle shelf, left **7** grapes **8** middle of all 3 shelves **9** various

Unit 106 Page 62

1 a Bedroom 2 b Bedroom 1 and bathroom c living area d laundry **2** various for e.g. a through the living area b past ;laundry through the living area c past Bedroom 2 d through living area past bathroom **3** various e.g. a from A towards B turn right at intersection, next intersection turn right b from C towards D turn right at intersection, next intersection turn left follow the path c from B at intersection turn left follow to D d from F at intersection turn left follow to C **4** various e.g. a 4 squares up and 1 square right b 2 squares up and 2 squares right c 1 square up and 4 squares right d 2 squares right **5** Bedroom 1 and Bedroom 3 **6** various e.g. through living area and pass laundry **7** various e.g. from E towards F, through 1st intersection then turn left and follow to G. **8** 4 squares up and 1 square right **9** various

Unit 107 Page 63

1 a ✶ b ▲ c ÷ d ♦ **2** a A4 b D4 c D2 d C1 **3** a Jo b Karen c Kylie d Neil **4** various e.g. a on Circle Court next to Andrew's house b Subtraction Street c at end of Less than Lane, opposite the train station d off Circle Court opposite the shop **5** % **6** B2 **7** Andrew **8** various e.g. Less than Lane, opposite the pool **9** e.g.

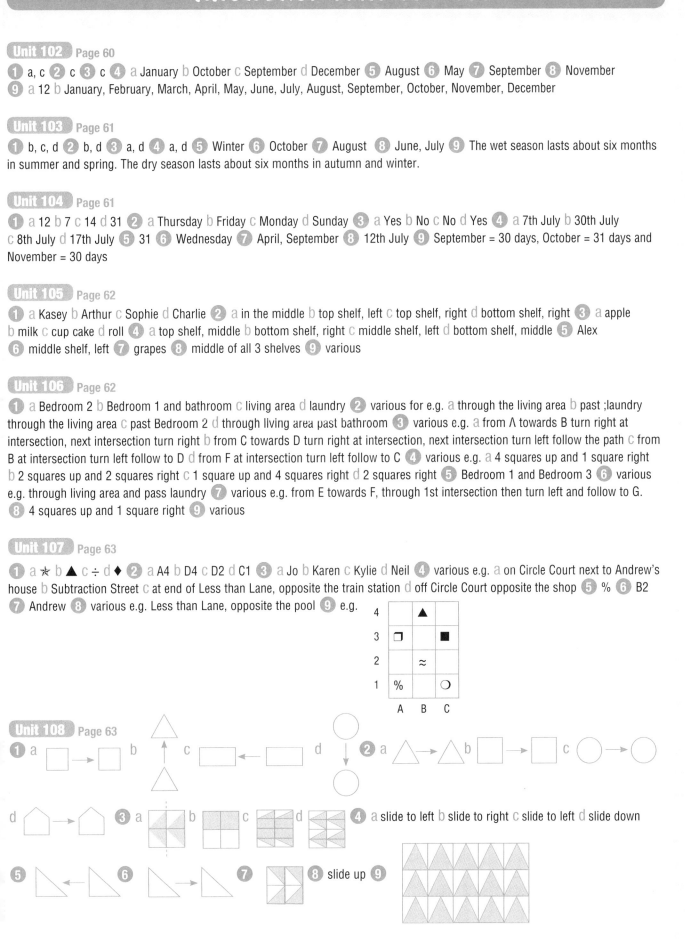

Unit 108 Page 63

1 a ☐→☐ b ↑▲ c ▭←▭ d ↓ **2** a △→△ b ☐→☐ c ○→○ d ⌂→⌂ **3** a b c d **4** a slide to left b slide to right c slide to left d slide down

5 **6** **7** **8** slide up **9**

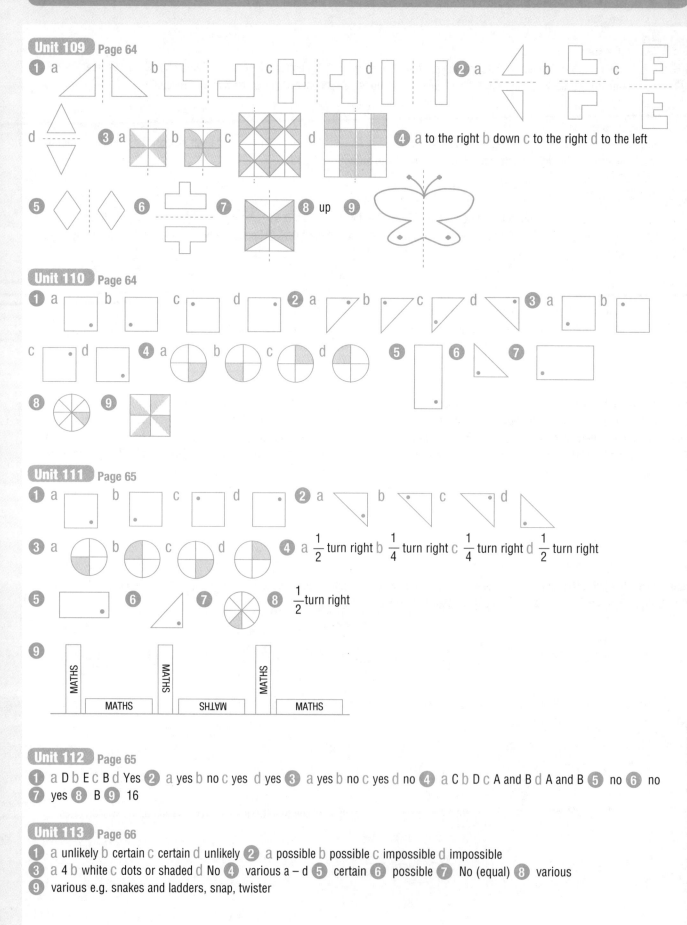

Unit 109 Page 64

1 a b c d 2 a b c

d 3 a b c d 4 a to the right b down c to the right d to the left

5 6 7 8 up 9

Unit 110 Page 64

1 a b c d 2 a b c d 3 a b

c d 4 a b c d 5 6 7

8 9

Unit 111 Page 65

1 a b c d 2 a b c d

3 a b c d 4 a $\frac{1}{2}$ turn right b $\frac{1}{4}$ turn right c $\frac{1}{4}$ turn right d $\frac{1}{2}$ turn right

5 6 7 8 $\frac{1}{2}$ turn right

9

MATHS MATHS MATHS
MATHS SHTAM MATHS

Unit 112 Page 65

1 a D b E c B d Yes 2 a yes b no c yes d yes 3 a yes b no c yes d no 4 a C b D c A and B d A and B 5 no 6 no
7 yes 8 B 9 16

Unit 113 Page 66

1 a unlikely b certain c certain d unlikely 2 a possible b possible c impossible d impossible
3 a 4 b white c dots or shaded d No 4 various a – d 5 certain 6 possible 7 No (equal) 8 various
9 various e.g. snakes and ladders, snap, twister

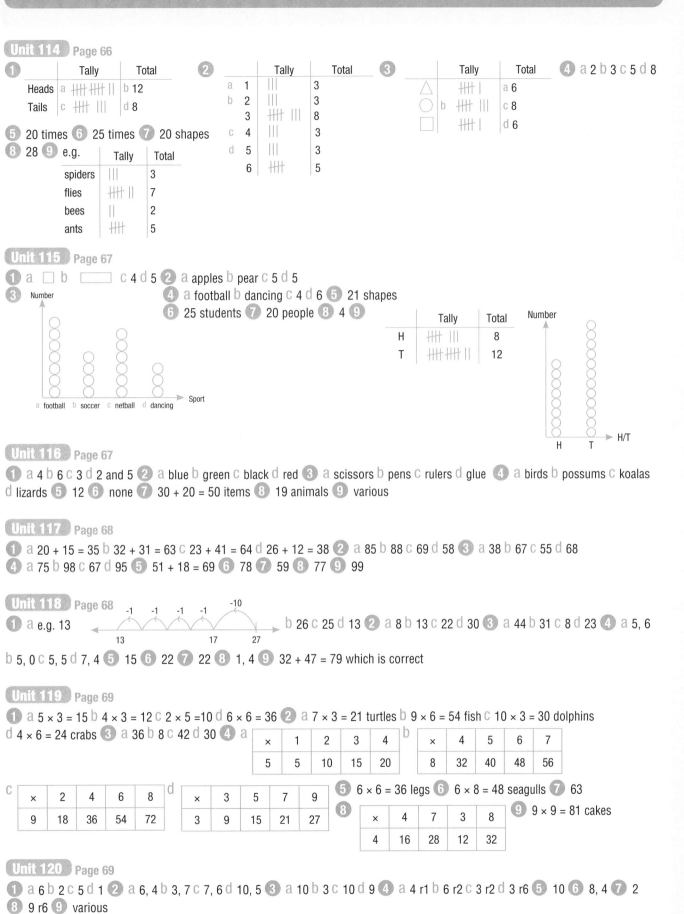

Unit 114 Page 66

1

	Tally	Total
Heads	a ||||| ||||| ||	b 12
Tails	c ||||| |||	d 8

2

		Tally	Total
a	1	|||	3
b	2	|||	3
	3										8
c	4	|||	3
d	5	|||	3
	6							5

3

		Tally	Total
△		|||||		a 6
○	b	||||| |||	c 8
□		|||||		d 6

4 a 2 b 3 c 5 d 8

5 20 times **6** 25 times **7** 20 shapes
8 28 **9** e.g.

	Tally	Total
spiders	|||	3
flies	||||| ||	7
bees	||	2
ants	|||||	5

Unit 115 Page 67

1 a □ b ▭ c 4 d 5 **2** a apples b pear c 5 d 5
3
4 a football b dancing c 4 d 6 **5** 21 shapes
6 25 students **7** 20 people **8** 4 **9**

	Tally	Total
H	||||| |||	8
T	||||| ||||| ||	12

Unit 116 Page 67

1 a 4 b 6 c 3 d 2 and 5 **2** a blue b green c black d red **3** a scissors b pens c rulers d glue **4** a birds b possums c koalas
d lizards **5** 12 **6** none **7** 30 + 20 = 50 items **8** 19 animals **9** various

Unit 117 Page 68

1 a 20 + 15 = 35 b 32 + 31 = 63 c 23 + 41 = 64 d 26 + 12 = 38 **2** a 85 b 88 c 69 d 58 **3** a 38 b 67 c 55 d 68
4 a 75 b 98 c 67 d 95 **5** 51 + 18 = 69 **6** 78 **7** 59 **8** 77 **9** 99

Unit 118 Page 68

1 a e.g. 13
b 26 c 25 d 13 **2** a 8 b 13 c 22 d 30 **3** a 44 b 31 c 8 d 23 **4** a 5, 6
b 5, 0 c 5, 5 d 7, 4 **5** 15 **6** 22 **7** 22 **8** 1, 4 **9** 32 + 47 = 79 which is correct

Unit 119 Page 69

1 a 5 × 3 = 15 b 4 × 3 = 12 c 2 × 5 = 10 d 6 × 6 = 36 **2** a 7 × 3 = 21 turtles b 9 × 6 = 54 fish c 10 × 3 = 30 dolphins
d 4 × 6 = 24 crabs **3** a 36 b 8 c 42 d 30 **4** a

×	1	2	3	4
5	5	10	15	20

b

×	4	5	6	7
8	32	40	48	56

c

×	2	4	6	8
9	18	36	54	72

d

×	3	5	7	9
3	9	15	21	27

5 6 × 6 = 36 legs **6** 6 × 8 = 48 seagulls **7** 63
8

×	4	7	3	8
4	16	28	12	32

9 9 × 9 = 81 cakes

Unit 120 Page 69

1 a 6 b 2 c 5 d 1 **2** a 6, 4 b 3, 7 c 7, 6 d 10, 5 **3** a 10 b 3 c 10 d 9 **4** a 4 r1 b 6 r2 c 3 r2 d 3 r6 **5** 10 **6** 8, 4 **7** 2
8 9 r6 **9** various

Review Tests Units 1–5   Page 70

1 D 2 D 3 True 4 True 5 46 6 seventy-three 7 36, 46, 67, 73 8 90 9 84 10 543 11 74 12 3, 4, 1, 2

Review Tests Units 6–10   Page 70

1 A 2 B 3 True 4 False 5 628 6 55, 58, 61, 64 7 300 + 20 + 7 8 | 4 | H | 0 | T | 7 | U | 9
10 1208 11 four thousand, two hundred and fifty-one 12 seven hundred and nineteen

Review Tests Units 11–16   Page 71

1 C 2 D 3 True 4 False 5 6 + 5 = 11 6 7 7 8, 13, 18 8 9 + 5 = 14 9 37 10
11 10 + 8 = 18 12 a 20 b 100 c 40 d 80

+	11	12	13	14
10	21	22	23	24

Review Tests Units 17–22   Page 71

1 D 2 B 3 False 4 True 5 9t + 7u 6

27 + 12 = 39

7

+	12	22	32	42
6	18	28	38	48

8 20 9 37 10 32 + 22 = 54 11 0, 8 12 5 + 13 + 21 = 39

Review Tests Units 23–28   Page 72

1 C 2 C 3 False 4 True 5 12 − 7 = 5 6 24 7 3
8

−	19	29	39	49
10	9	19	29	39

9 15 − 8 = 7 10 72 − 10 = 62 11

20 − 7 = 13

12 4, 4, 13

Review Tests Units 29–33   Page 72

1 B 2 B 3 True 4 False 5 3t + 2u 6 53 7 27 − 23 = 4 cupcakes 8 7, 4 9 13, 13, 74 10 40, 41 11 76 − 33 = 43
12 64 − 41 = 23 twenty-three

Review Tests Units 34–38   Page 73

1 A 2 C 3 False 4 True 5 4 × 4 = 16 6 True 7 10, 30 8

9

= 14

10 35 11 4 + 4 + 4 + 4 + 4 12 3 × 5

Review Tests Units 39–46   Page 73

1 C 2 A 3 False 4 True 5 6 × 3 = 18 6

×	3	6	8	1
5	15	30	40	5

7 42 8 6, 24 9 various e.g. 5 × 3

10 twenty-eight 11 various e.g.

12 9 × 6 = 54, she could go 6 times

ANSWERS: Review Test Units 47–84

Review Tests Units 47–52 Page 74

① A ② D ③ False ④ True ⑤ ⑥ 8 ÷ 2 = 4
0 2 4 6 8

⑦ 14 ÷ 2 = 7 ⑧ 5 ⑨ 10 r1 10 groups and 1 left over ⑩ various ⑪ e.g. 20 ÷ 5 = 4 ⑫ 5 cards

Review Tests Units 53–57 Page 74

① D ② B ③ True ④ False ⑤ 400 ⑥ 69 e.g. 46 + 20 + 3 = 69 ⑦ 16, 36 ⑧ 4 ⑨ False ⑩ 61 − 44 = 17
⑪ 500 + 400 = 900 ⑫ various 2 r4

Review Tests Units 58–61 Page 75

① C ② A ③ True ④ True ⑤ 57, 59, 61 ⑥ 66 + 25 = 91 items ⑦ 80, 77, 74, 71 ⑧ 150, 160, 170 ⑨ various
⑩ start at 100, count backwards by 5 ⑪ 16 ⑫ fifty-seven, fifty-nine, sixty-one

Review Tests Units 62–64 Page 75

① B ② A ③ False ④ True ⑤

+	10	20	30	40
11	21	31	41	51

⑥ 15, 18, 21, 24 ⑦ start at 40 and count backwards by 3

⑧ 48 − 25 = 23 pencils ⑨ 60 ⑩ various, answer 6 ⑪ 24, 48, 96 ⑫ 10 + 12 + 6 + 2 = 30 animals on the farm

Review Tests Units 65–68 Page 76

① B ② C ③ False ④ True ⑤ 2, 4 ⑥ e.g. ⑦ e.g. ⑧ $\frac{2}{8}$ ⑨ e.g. ⑩ e.g.
⑪ ⑫ e.g.

Review Tests Units 69–71 Page 76

① D ② A ③ True ④ False ⑤ ⑥ $\frac{5}{8}$ ⑦ e.g. ⑧ $\frac{1}{10}$ $\frac{8}{10}$ $\frac{10}{10}$

⑨ e.g. ⑩ seven tenths ⑪ $\frac{1}{10}$ $\frac{3}{10}$ $\frac{10}{10}$ ⑫ eight tenths

Review Tests Units 72–74 Page 77

① D ② A ③ False ④ True ⑤ 5c, 20c, 50c, $2 ⑥ $2 ⑦ $80 ⑧ $7.75 ⑨ $15 ⑩
⑪ $53.55 ⑫ e.g. $6.45 = $2 + $2 + $2 + 20c + 20c + 5c

Review Tests Units 75–78 Page 77

① C ② B ③ False ④ True ⑤ △, ◯ △, ⑥ 4 + 9 = 13 stars ⑦ e.g. twelve stars takeaway seven stars = five stars
⑧ circle, triangle, star, repeated 2 times ⑨ start at 60 and count forwards by 4 ⑩ 19 − 9 = 10 cars ⑪ six ⑫ various

Review Tests Units 79–84 Page 78

① D ② A ③ True ④ False ⑤ rectangle – 4 sides, opposites are equal length ⑥ △ ⑦ ◯ ⑧ circle ⑨ cube ⑩ 9
⑪ rhombus ⑫

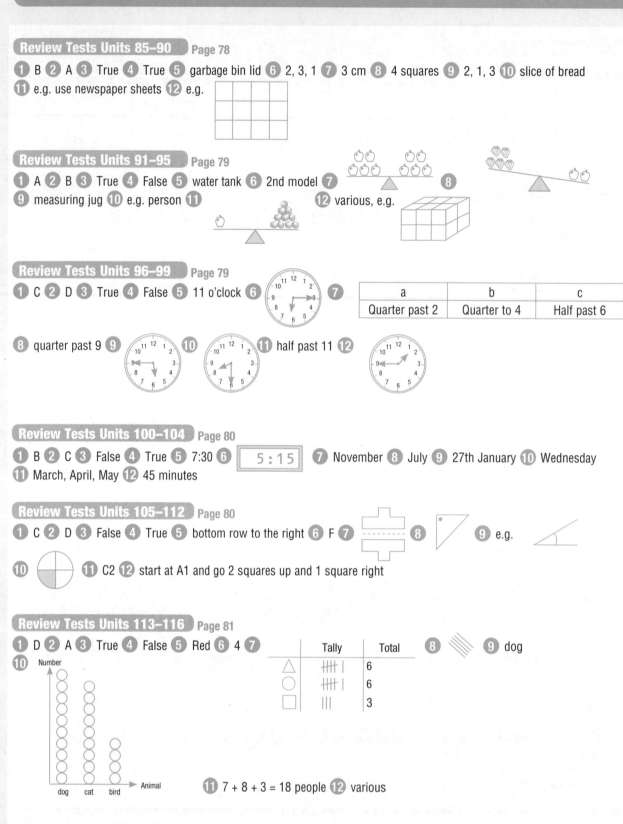

Review Tests Units 85–90 Page 78

1 B **2** A **3** True **4** True **5** garbage bin lid **6** 2, 3, 1 **7** 3 cm **8** 4 squares **9** 2, 1, 3 **10** slice of bread
11 e.g. use newspaper sheets **12** e.g.

Review Tests Units 91–95 Page 79

1 A **2** B **3** True **4** False **5** water tank **6** 2nd model **7**
9 measuring jug **10** e.g. person **11** **12** various, e.g.

Review Tests Units 96–99 Page 79

1 C **2** D **3** True **4** False **5** 11 o'clock **6** **7**

a	b	c
Quarter past 2	Quarter to 4	Half past 6

8 quarter past 9 **9** **10** **11** half past 11 **12**

Review Tests Units 100–104 Page 80

1 B **2** C **3** False **4** True **5** 7:30 **6** 5:15 **7** November **8** July **9** 27th January **10** Wednesday
11 March, April, May **12** 45 minutes

Review Tests Units 105–112 Page 80

1 C **2** D **3** False **4** True **5** bottom row to the right **6** F **7** **8** **9** e.g.
10 **11** C2 **12** start at A1 and go 2 squares up and 1 square right

Review Tests Units 113–116 Page 81

1 D **2** A **3** True **4** False **5** Red **6** 4 **7**

	Tally	Total
△	ⵀⵀ l	6
○	ⵀⵀ l	6
□	lll	3

8 **9** dog
10

11 7 + 8 + 3 = 18 people **12** various

Review Tests Units 117–120 Page 81

1 D **2** D **3** True **4** False **5** 22 + 35 = 57 **6** 42 − 21 = 21 **7**

×	4	7	8	1
3	12	21	24	3

8 10 **9** 7, 4
10 3 × 5 = 15 **11** 31 chickens **12** 7, 5